CONTENTS

Foreword

Introduction. About this book and who it Is aimed at.

Chapter 1. The journey into breakdown and the path to forgiveness.

Chapter 2. I get to recovery then fall in love.

Chapter 3. Trying to describe it.

Chapter4. Medication. Will you or won't you?

Chapter 4a. A practical equation and a guide for carers.

Chapter 5. Please breathe.

Chapter 6 Unlock your life jigsaw.

Chapter7. The Vacuums.

Chapter 7a. An exercise for physical trauma.

Chapter 8 . Self- love and healing; The spiritual way to help recovery and renewal.

Chapter 9 Nutrition; Section 1. Theory; the gut, the thyroid. Section2. Practical help; foraging and healthy alternative mood boosters and calmers.

Chapter 10. What I Have become; Inner me, visions, spirits and Simon.

Chapter 11. The Bridge.

Chapter 12. Perceptions of mental help and the modern world.

Chapter 12a. Note to parents.

Disclaimer

Please note this guide is for informative purposes only. I am not a medical professional and can only convey my experiences. Any changes you make must be done under guidance of your medical professional or health care professional.

The use of alternative medicine and nutrition is a complicated science and must be respected that way.

Always try any changes with the help and love from those around. Within these pages you may find a change or practice that will benefit you but please do it cautiously and with patience and not alone.

Morag Morgan (2021)

Foreword

by Beth Yabsley

"I know the bottom, she says. I know it with my great tap root:

It is what you fear.

I do not fear it: I have been there."

'Elm' by Sylvia Plath, 1962.

Morag is my friend, although I haven't known her very long. I absolutely love 'The Breakdown That Made Me' but I know I'd love it as a book and recognize its importance within its subject matter whether I knew Morag or not.

Mental health is a topic I've read around widely and voraciously since my teenage years. It was a lightbulb moment for me reading 'Prozac Nation' by the wonderful Elizabeth Wurtzel for the first time. I've spoken to many people about Morag's book; the opportunity of this dialogue is a wonderful thing in itself. Thirty years ago (when I had just hit my teenage years) it would have been less likely that people would be talking so openly about how they feel in the hope of making themselves feel better.

It's certainly more commonplace to talk about 'wellness' so conversely it should be just as easy to talk about the flipside of this. It's liberating to be able to do so, not to mention potentially lifesaving as it means you can receive the support you deserve.

I've struggled with depression, anxiety and self-esteem issues on and off for decades. My parents have been the most supportive parents I could ever have wished for.

I've been called 'mental' when in fact my mental health was in crisis; the word 'mental' used to detrimental effect can be so damaging. This is why Morag's book is so necessary: de-stigmatising these journeys from breakdowns to recovery and beyond needs to continue and to embed itself into society.

I'm sure you'll love reading Morag's book as much as I did; I don't think you can fail to find it touching and uplifting despite the subject matter. It's not an easy read in the sense that it's emotive, raw and searingly honest at times. However, it is also consistently kind and passionate about providing hope for others.

It's both a bearing of a woman's soul and an extensive toolkit of ways to help others move forward towards a happier place and version of themselves. It does this in a variety of approaches. As you read her book you will find out that at times Morag's struggled with the 'one size fits all' attitude to her illness and as such this book provides a plethora of different constructive approaches to help – there should be something in there for everyone to try.

Of course, there is no quick solution, magic cure or way of fixing mental illness, suffering and pain. If there were, it would be tremendous, but this book gives you a fighting chance to be better prepared when the mind (and also the body) become incredibly uncomfortable and painful to inhabit. Upon recovery, the advice will help your ability to maintain physical, emotional and spiritual health.

What this book does offer is a series of ways, which are easily accessible and most are free, to support yourself and others holistically to ensure that you are as robust as possible to deal with the curved balls that life can throw at us.

We can't control what happens in life, but we can control the extent of our reactions. We are likely to be less emotionally reactive when we are healthy in the three ways referenced above.

This doesn't have to be a constant state of being and we shouldn't aim to look after ourselves perfectly. Personally, I try to focus on progress not perfection. Seeking perfection will only be detrimental to our mental health. The times I have felt most stuck is when I simply don't know what to do to make myself feel better.

This book gives lots of things you can do for yourself, or someone else if you are caring for them, to improve your /their mental health. The ideas in the book are by no means exhaustive, but I'm confident in the assertion that there is something in there for everyone. The breadth of information that Morag gives (which crucially has all been 'lived' by her) empowers us to do the best that we can for ourselves and others to maintain mental equilibrium. This is, quite simply, one of the kindest books I've ever read.

It's also very much a book of its time, I'm a big believer that literature is best read in context. Morag references the topsy turvy economy of the country we're in right now and gives societal insights which demonstrate how when you feel stuck you need choices, and the state of the economy and recent governmental decisions have stripped people of choices, which is one of the most dehumanizing positions to be in.

I'm sure that Morag's book is one you'll return to. It is designed to be read as chronological prose with her poetry framing the end of each chapter. It transcends this though with the fact that it does work across genres to act as a reference book / manual for wellbeing and much more.

I'd like to thank one healthcare professional who was instrumental in helping me feel better – Dr. P was professional kindness personified when I needed it.

I'd like to dedicate this foreword to my beautiful cousin Kim Ann Marie Yardley 26.12.1981 – 24.07.2020. She left this world too soon.

Rest in Peace Kim, lots of love.

Introduction and Acknowledgements:

"You are the sky, everything else; it's just the weather"

Pema Chodron.

About this book and who it is aimed at.

In 2014 I had a severe breakdown. I was given some heavy anti-anxiety and anti-depressant drugs which catapulted me further into a seemingly endless terrifying pit that lasted for nearly 2 years.

This book is written to all of those interested or experiencing mental health difficulties to offer you hope and light for recovery.

Writing this book has sometimes made me anxious when I recalled the memory of these events. However, I have learned to love the little girl who was so afraid inside me for so long. Chapter 11, The Bridge, explains that this is an ongoing process.

The poems, some angry, some hopeless, some hopeful, are an expression of what I felt in that moment and originally the poems were just for me, but I have realised that the words inside captured the prison I was in and that others may recognise or relate to.

You must come to understand that I am now at peace and thriving. So, whilst my journey was personal, it also presents themes that are universal as Tessa Goldhawk (a Hypnotherapist I was treated by) in her beautiful book 'A Rose to A Sick Friend' conveys the suffering we endure but also captures the mindset that helps us accept illness and often the new person we become after;

'Each suffering we undergo may seem at the time to weaken our bodies; but it is a great opportunity to strengthen our souls; our inner centre; our wisdom and our contact with source. Illness is one of the ways we are given to learn about ourselves, and to grow. If we let it, it can be moving and inspiring journey' (page 10)

My aim for this publication is to invigorate you rather than make you sad; but I can't control your emotions just as you can't mine. We are all living in a series of borrowed cells ignited with many different stories which ultimately have an effect on how we perceive our experiences.

What you may recognise however, **is the transformation I took from terrifying hopelessness to a freedom I have never known** and a platform from which I thrive rather than create demise.

The words and poems in this book are my experience, some express anger for some of those people around me at the time who could not help and am sure felt helpless themselves. Other poems reflect the pain of being a Mother as resembling a tiger watching her cub play whilst she is pacing and trapped in a cage of anxiety desperate to be there for her little one.

There is practical advice and raw ramblings but the message is simple; **you can recover.**

When I realised out of pure impossibility there was a light and that I could survive I felt it was important to write about this experience. More importantly I thought it was important **I spoke for the people who are often not listened to well enough when they are in so much pain.** Their opinion can be misheard or undermined because of the mental illness status they carry with them.

The following chapters compartmentalise under specific titles so we can deal with each and every challenge we face when our life falls apart. I cover my experiences in order to highlight the issues I faced, as you may well recognise them in your own.

I try to offer practical solutions to help move the situation forward. Some advice may not be achievable straight away because when we fall apart the first things we need are very simple; safety, connection, kindness and time.

With regard to those who couldn't help; truth is I'm not sure I would have been able to help me either.

All is forgiven, and as one person kindly said fairly recently, "your illness wore us out," despite only visiting me a handful of times and that was enough for them; seriously I was bad.

However, **the illness is not mine like the trauma you experience is not yours either.** It is something that happened to me from which I have recovered. I'm sure it did wear them out in their minds and their words may be frustrations of being locked in their world of demands, whilst feeling helpless to improve other's lives.

If you do feel frustrated at someone who is in mental turmoil try not to project your frustrations at the illness a clear 'no win' for anybody; imagine whatever you feel they are feeling much worse.

This is a common reaction but is actually abusive and unhelpful to the person who is suffering and I hope to educate close ones and care givers to approach this person differently, in a way which benefits both parties.

Many visited on irregular terms, when small regular offerings of help are much more effective and prevent 'burn out' and provide structure for the afflicted person.

It also prevents the person trying to help to not feel guilty for desperately wanting to abandon the sinking ship before they go down with it too. **It is constructive help agreed on both sides with boundaries in place that seems to be a 'win win' for both parties (see Chapter 4A).**

I have learned I must let myself have those expressions otherwise they will ruminate and become toxic. They might not be valid to others, but they are mine and I honour them and give them the opportunity to flow and dissolve.

There is no coincidence that the word emotion has 'motion' incorporated in it; accepting, acknowledging a feeling and letting it move within our bodies is as effective as a parent reassuring their child that they do not need to be afraid.

Whilst recovered, I am without a doubt vulnerable and not perfect and that is our beauty **and the acknowledgement of these very imperfections is our power.**

I told one person, asking for advice recently, that their pursuit for perfection meant they constantly berated themselves; this is fruitless and has the opposite effects it sets out to achieve.

I can't make you love yourself for all you are, including the imperfections, but I am hoping this book will guide you on that path, for self-love is one of the keys to recovery and contentment. **You are not your past; many of the finest teach us that, in this moment, there is every opportunity to change everything.**

This book also flags up the gaps in our society for people who drop by the wayside and how our society is not set up to cushion them. The mental health drugs the NHS provide sometimes help, if unmonitored (which often they are) can also be a monster, making an already seemingly catastrophic situation unimaginably horrific.

It reflects how mental health is seen differently as a journey or gift in some tribal environments. **Taking away the stigma that is attached to mental health in our society and giving hope for a journey many have to take during our lives.**

I hope this book breaks this stigma. We are living in a frail world where opening our hearts and minds is essential for our survival.

Then of course there is **time**; our limitations we have in slotting others in need into our busy lives because of course for the victim of a breakdown, time will stop.

Somehow in making everything less time consuming we have made less time; time to heal, time to nurture others that suffer. We are in a routine that neither allows for fault or can tolerate it, and our mental health gets pushed aside, misunderstood and lost.

By creating more technological connection we have become spiritually disconnected. We want to offer all the solutions in an Amazon next day delivery package to those afflicted with a breakdown. We have become impatient with those who need our time.

The truth is breakdowns don't follow any chronology they are created by physical (including hormonal) and emotional imbalances, overloading these systems suddenly, over months or even years. Their emergence is complex and their recovery requires patience, support, connection and time.

Whilst I appreciate Doctors; I don't always think that labelling someone with a specific mental health issue is always helpful in every case. Simply put, this is because the journey of having got there may lie in many layers and once there, to be labelled may provide a prison and prescription rather than a path out.

The same goes for offering medication a 'one pill fits all' scenario; the uses of which have rocketed in over the last two decades. I cannot stress enough that these chemicals are massive game changers in your brain and the complexities of how a person gets into this situation cannot always be nulled or resolved with a chemical and indeed the drug's reaction can be catastrophic for some. More tragically for many cases it is even acknowledged or recognised that the drug had a hand in their further downfall.

If you have been on chemicals for years, you cannot just come off them either because you have asked a chemical to change a whole part of your brain. Patience and time are required as well as monitoring to make these steps. If you come off too quickly even up to three months later, **return of symptoms can actually be withdrawals from the drug.** This is why taking medication needs more understanding and definitive processes because without understanding the way in which they work, many get trapped in taking an anti-anxiety or anti-depressant pharmaceutical for the rest of their lives that they do not necessarily need to be on. If you are thinking of coming off mental health medication, then in chapter 4, I offer advice on how to sensibly do this to get the best result.

Medication has become a 'quick fix' to our busy lives but sadly it is not always the answer. Communities continue to fragment as we place more demands upon ourselves. Also, the loss of connection and destruction of our natural world, our source, has made us all vulnerable to mental health difficulties. As Jim Carrey so perfectly puts it:

"Society is collapsing, and people are starting to recognize that the reason they feel like they're mentally ill is that they're living in a system that's not designed to suit the human spirit."

If our society here in the UK had wanted to develop and understand mental health treatments they would not have significantly systematically underfunded it. This in itself shows how unimportant recovery from mental health is to them and why pharmaceutical treatments are placed upon people as a quick fix solution so they can 'carry on as normal.'

Without long term strategies to recovery other than medication, it is clearly a 'numbing' and not a 'healing' approach that has been adopted in these times of underfunding and disconnection. [Mentalhealthfundingreport20.pdf (tuc.org.uk)](Mentalhealthfundingreport20.pdf)

As well as limitations in society, this book gives an understanding of how to trace some of the tapestry of our own emotional journey; without necessarily having to delve deep into trauma (although sometimes this can help), **but by taking apart the cloth and understanding how it was woven together we then get a greater understanding and respect for its creation.**

In doing so, and ultimately surviving a breakdown, we suddenly realise the tapestry is our own; it is not for the utilisation of others, it is for you to love and the **view of yourself comes then internally, not externally from others.**

This is a significant transformation this is the great shift to self- love something which I was not accustomed to till after experiencing a breakdown.

Before we can even begin to look at our own emotional tapestry though we need others to simply make us feel safe; we need to be held and loved. We need to be **nurtured** and this is another word you will become familiar with within this book for if we are vulnerable then we need nurture.

I will never be able to describe the terror and vulnerability I felt sometimes 24/7, **I am amazed I survived but I am writing this because I did and you can too. Inside us all is the child we need to listen to. In Chapter 4a I offer a practical equation for First Aid of a breakdown. SNCS; Safety, Nurture, Connection, Structure.**

For those who have survived a breakdown (because you can and will), often they describe a new self; it is sometimes like the breakdown has rebuilt them in a better way and this is the hope I will give to you through this book and an understanding of how loved ones can get through it with you.

For those who have suffered all your lives; I respect and honour you for your bravery and hope this book can also throw light onto your situation too. If you can always think outside your label (see Phil Borges chapter 12) whilst you are well you may still find your answer   for you have been brave enough for this long and I hope I can offer you a door to less pain.

Despite modern limitations extraordinary people came to help me. They ignored time constraints and offered me their home, their availability and their trust.

Within this environment I was able to start healing because at last I felt safe. These people were often people who had suffered themselves, were naturally kind or had developed their kindness from life challenges...they were my nurturing arms.

For none of us are perfect and sometimes within those imperfection and vulnerabilities lies our beauty.

Finally, I want to say that this book offers a mixture of my story practical advice on diet and medication but what really stands out or the light I give to you is **Chapter 6 and 7; our jigsaws and vacuums** *because once we understand and acknowledge our pain* *we are no longer a slave to the past; just an observer of how you have responded to it.*

If your anxiety is high right now it may be worth starting at Chapter 5 for the practical advice as 1 to 4 are really the details of how I got into a severe state and may be quite harrowing.

Along with nurturing and being kind to your body these approaches may be the key to your recovery. All Parents please look at Chapter 12a 'A note for parents' because not only are your children your teachers the way you approach them will have a major impact on their later life and opinions they have on themselves that can either limit them or make them thrive.

Acknowledgements; Those who were unconditionally there and that I owe my life to: Simon (who I literally owe my life to), Frazer, Mike, Jan , Sharon (my old neighbour), my dear friend Colin, Kirsty who through kindness opened a very important door to my recovery..thank you!, Laurian, Denise, Marie ; the last three my motley crew of the kindest dedicated friends that still remain a strong force of support...also Katie G, Andy (my therapist) , Mick , Rachel, Helen; both my childhood friends, my Mom(*) and family, Jama, Johanna H for giving me a regular spot of your love and time and Ruth G for having me over for dinner without knowing me that well, but knowing I was in pain, Holly, Mary, Jo Ross, Rose Ross and just the kind Ross family in general! The two Hannahs, Fi, Claire, my neighbours Paul and Helen, my foraging friend Raymond who taught me how to be healed by nature again. Steph my new friend and poet who made me feel my poems were worth it. Also my editor Beth Yabsley who came into my life at exactly the right time with so much enthusiasm.

(*) I will always use 'Mom' throughout the book, I'm from the Midlands. I have been mocked for this but simply; I don't care it is me and who I am. There you go; proof is in the pudding. I don't have to rely on others to value myself anymore.

Thank you to my new friends for teaching me that family does not have to be blood and for giving your energy and time without expectation or conditions of anything in return other than my wellbeing. Thank you to my partner Matthew who is probably one of the most devoted, kindest people I know.

Workers who got it…. Helen from the mental Health team I don't even know your surname but you changed the whole course of my medication nightmare you are simply a lovely human being; thank you so much. Doctor K who finally heard what I was saying and changed my meds, Norman from Mind who constantly spoke to my doctor with concerns, Tessa (Hypnotherapist), Agnes from Addaction for finally hearing me also, Maryellen the Chiropractor for offering me free treatments and such kindness and always having hope that I would survive and Tim S a great herbalist who offered me many of his hours without charge desperately trying to find solutions and helping me get off Diazepam.

Jo you are a great worker and so meant to be in this profession but don't always be bound by your Psychiatrist's advice, sometimes Psychiatrists are the least connected to the client; qualifications aren't everything.

This book is dedicated to those people and all the genuine carers and nurses out there who try so hard to help people in a world that has lost its way.

Of course though this book is dedicated to my son; the bonds that hold us so close to our children were powerful enough to keep me here in this world. Thank you my beautiful son and even though I couldn't care what anyone else thinks, as a Mother I still hold shame for falling apart and I hope that you forgive me.

So, hold on to your breeches folks because all I can tell you is 'nothing stays the same,' there is always change and the only way you're heading is up!

For all of us though: slow down, give time and kindness and learn to re -live, re- love and see your light again.

A text from my safe friend

For all my life

I have focused on things that

Make me feel safe

And to that degree I was in control

I now realise, what a waste

Of precious time and error all that was!

It gets you nowhere

And leaves you with nothing!

I know now that people are everything

Where are we without others?

But we are all just temporary

Here today; gone literally tomorrow.

You have always realised the crucial importance of others!

That's why you are struggling so dreadfully now.

So rest assured all your priorities are in the right place

Us others are just waiting for you

To come home.

By Colin Stapleton my beautiful friend.

Chapter 1

<u>The journey to this book and a path to forgiveness.</u>

My name is Morag; I am 49 years old and am lucky to be alive; but somehow I survived.

I am writing this book in hope that others will understand and reach out to people who undergo severe mental health collapse or as some put it a 'nervous breakdown'.

When this unexpectedly became me, it was terrifying that people did not seem to understand how to help me go through this process in life. There is no doubt about it; it is a very difficult situation to be in for both parties.

Claire Weekes' within her book "Self Help For Your Nerves" (1962) offers a pioneer approach that recognised the extremities of anxiety and fear. When I became ill this was the only book I read that seemed to describe the severity of what my body was experiencing. It is quite outdated now and I don't necessarily agree with the medical solutions (which included Benzodiazepines) she describes within it.

However, I totally agree with Weekes' description of the disabling condition of sudden severe mental relapses. Her work at the time was so forward thinking in the recognition of this condition that it actually caused controversy; somebody had finally identified severe anxiety and depression as a very serious life-threatening condition.

Weekes preferred to call it 'Nervous Illness' and she educates us that 'Nervous illness' is not necessarily always caused by a flawed personality as is often portrayed or even trauma but can be a combination of fear avoidance and an over sensitive nervous system. Controversially she offered recovery to this debilitating illness and pioneered CBT (Cognitive Behavioural Therapy).

Now this book won't lead you to CBT as a solution necessarily and it won't get hooked on one therapy but it will take you on a journey to find your solution.

What is implicit in Weekes's book is that people in this extreme state should not be alone and should be nurtured like a physically ill patient and that time and nurture was needed for recovery. She recognises that most people who experience a breakdown will find normal day to day activities difficult and even frightening.

Unfortunately, I did find myself alone at some points. Some people were there to help at times but I had to bargain and organise and sometimes beg for their company. The extremities of my condition made it exhausting for them. If their life already had stress, being with me was a total drain on their energy. For this reason, I have put together an equation of First Aid for a breakdown described in Chapter 4a that may be able to help both parties to make a plan that provides a suitable solution and foundation for recovery.

Later in my journey some people responded to me miraculously. Furthermore, some new turned up in the middle of my nightmare and committed themselves selflessly which in itself was a gift for my recovery.

We often hear on the radio a voice sadly professing that there has been "another **preventable** suicide" **but we are so far from preventing suicide in resources, understanding, consciousness and connection** and we appear to have become more fragmented as a society than ever before.

In fact, by underfunding our mental health services and not prioritising this vital part of our functioning society, we have sent, what could have been a dynamic progressive support system/centres back to an outdated game of **Pharmaceutical Russian Roulette.**

This means unwanted side effects get unreported or missed and people are left alone or sent home with brain altering drugs that could well be a danger to their vulnerable state.

Prince Harry ran a campaign to tell people to speak out about mental health; especially for men who are less likely to talk about feelings of depression and aloneness and are **3.5 times** more likely to commit suicide (1) ;4590 male compared to 1391 female **(2018)** Although the lowest rated group under 25s suicide rates are rising significantly and this time more so among females.
(https://www.ons.gov.uk/peoplepopulationandcommunity/birthsdeathsandmarriages/deaths/bulletins/suicidesintheunitedkingdom/2018registrations).

In 2018, 71 ex-soldiers committed suicide because of PTSD. Perhaps Governments entering young men and women into these tragic 'no win' violent conflicts should be held to account, but instead because of a skeleton mental health service, soldiers with PTSD too often end up on the streets.

Now in 2021 we are just recovering from a 'Lockdown' (although I am not banking on it!), I don't need to explain what that is because day in and day out 'Lockdown' and 'Covid' have been drilled into our heads from the media. The very words have become ingrained in our everyday conversations and the effect of this brain programming won't be understood for years. We know the use of this constant patter in our heads creates fear worry inflammation and disease…dis - ease. How Anxiety Can Trigger Your Inflammation (Plus: What Foods to Avoid) (paleohacks.com)

What has become apparent as a result of 'locking down' is that we have increased suicidal thoughts and depression and this comes back to CONNECTION and NURTURE for without this care our souls become disembodied. • 'The dual pandemic' of suicide and COVID-19: A biopsychosocial narrative of risks and prevention (nih.gov)

I however did speak out and found a society and culture unable to cater to, or hear my cries. I was abandoned by many, not from their own choosing but because they couldn't cope.

In my deep despair I came to learn that some of my issues were abandonment and I came to re-live this feeling in a horrific way because those closest to me were gone.

Some of the worst decisions were made for me by those on the top tier of the NHS. Psychiatrists, Doctors prescribed drugs for me and left me unmonitored and suicidal; these decisions nearly cost me my life.

I remember often hearing through my compressed terrified head the terms 'Overstretched and underfunded' when I asked if I could go to hospital I was almost laughed at. **Despite feeling suicidal, having written several suicide notes, not sleeping and needing intense assessment I was not deemed a serious case.**

In Cornwall, which has a particularly bad funding in mental health, as a severe mental health case (Severe Agitated Depression diagnosis) I couldn't go to hospital, there was no hospital available for me. I was allocated a fortnightly visit. Go back 10 years or more and community mental health hospitals would have had a bed for me if only to keep me safe and assess me. Not only that, I could have taken myself along and checked myself in for an assessment.

Yes, you did read that correctly; someone **severely agitated and suicidal gets a fortnightly visit**. This is a terrifying prospect for a person in so much pain at the most critical intervention time.

I begged the Doctors to send me to a hospital but they said my case was not severe enough. My case was so severe that for a long time after I still found suicide notes tucked away around the house; too painful to read even now.

Simply what they meant by my case was not severe enough, is mental health hospitals do not exist anymore: they are now holding centres for the extreme cases so in my case would have 'made me worse,' according to Doctors and Psychiatrists assessing me.

The time and energy needed to assess and monitor me just was not there. I became an inconvenience to a society that I had trusted and felt safe in all my life. (*)

- 1990s MH hospitals in England and Wales; Patients could check themselves in if they didn't feel safe; like taking someone or yourself to A and E because you have broken a bone. Now some government officials have systematically withdrawn these safety nets and thrown away the key to these hospitals. What they class a severe is somewhere off the scale. Talk to families who have lost loved ones to suicide and let them tell you how no hospital beds were available or they were not classed as' severe' enough. Myself, my dear friend Sonny, two young teenagers and many others along the way. A pandemic of another kind; austerity and cuts to the social system lack of care for those who could not afford The Priory.
https://www.independent.co.uk/life-style/health-and-families/health-news/mental-hospital-closure-plan-is-condemned-
https://www.bmj.com/bmj/section-pdf/187386?path=%2Fbmj%2F343%2F7833%2FHead_to_Head.full.pdf

The medication issue is only part of this book and I am not going to spend the whole book being angry at people and throwing blame; most of these people were working in a very limited system and with lack of time to assess and monitor and consequently mistakes are ultimately made.

This is amplified by the fact that there is an unwillingness (and still stigmas) to acknowledge the needs of a mentally afflicted patient because their view can be misunderstood or distorted because of the broken platform they are coming from. Some of the poems in this book express these frustrations of not being heard.

I learned as part of my recovery that often people can only act and react with the life tools they have been given: **add to that a world that has made time its enemy and the result is a deadly equation.**

People bury their heads back into their busy lives and we can all justify this. Heard of the expression 'well you just have to look after yourself,' or 'My hands are tied,' but what are they tied with?

In close knit communities the support would have been very different but now, with fragmented individual pods of money earning teams this connection has been cut as capitalism and its focus on profit soar, but at what cost?

Perhaps the increasing use of anti- depressants is an indication that this system has lost the human spirit along the way and is simply not working.

In chapter 12, I look at tribal responses to mental health and their responses which are very different.

Finally, recovery requires forgiveness of others which is what I am still doing and why I am writing this book.

Forgiveness is essential part of recovery; it sets us free.

A beautiful example of this is spoken by Richard Moore, recalling his childhood in Derry when he got shot by a British Soldier at 10 years of age and was sadly blinded.

He tells Patrick Kielty on his show *'My Dad, the Peace Deal and Me'* that he had forgiven the man who shot him way before he had met him.

Kielty asks Moore how he came to forgive such an act (after losing his own Father to terrorism). Moore says he wouldn't dream of telling Kielty he needs to forgive his father's murderers, the hurt will always remain but he replies 'What forgiveness does it allows **you to let go**; it's not about the other person in my view.'

Moore spent his life helping children injured in wars worldwide from his charity 'Children in The Crossfire.' Forgiveness did set him free. (2)https://www.bbc.co.uk/news/uk-northern-ireland-foyle-west-43741785. You tube 'My Dad, The Peace Deal and Me.' (minutes38 to 40).

I have to own my own shit too for this breakdown but the experience was sadly a cauldron full of misunderstanding, misdiagnosis, mismanagement and fear from those who just couldn't handle me.

Now, I involve myself in many activities I would never have done before having a breakdown including: writing this book, setting up a business, public speaking, involving myself in environmental projects, foraging and more. My world is more boundless than it has ever been yet I am probably more empathic, reflective and quieter; although not everyone will agree with that last one.

Before this all happened, I looked strong on the outside but was incredibly lacking self-worth within and the journey you are on with me in this book will help you achieve the opposite. You will get to know you better than any other time in your life **for through this** *monumental fall I had learned to love myself.*

I view things differently now I reserve my time for those who deserve my time, because that as you will discover is one of two human gems we have now; the other is kindness.

I undertook many therapies and hardly any worked. So please don't despair if a therapy isn't working right now. Keep on soldiering on because there is a very high chance you will recover and sometimes the nurture and feeling safe has to come before any therapy, indeed as you continue to read you will realise that in some cultures what you are experiencing now will be your strength and gift in the future...*hold on my dear suffering friends, hold on!*

My hope to you is that everything changes and *'this will all pass'* these words were sometimes all I had to cling onto.

The depth of despair I reached matched the joy I gained on recovery; at the source of my recovery was a very strong motivation; a beautiful boy who needed his Mother. A Mother who teaches her son everyday how to honour his own feelings and not disregard them.

Please feel sadness, feel anger, let it all run through you and know it will pass, don't hold onto them either. Accept them and you let them move. Repeat them, hold onto them without change and your body becomes them and that is when our mental health can skip out of control.

Remember again that 'Emotion' separated spells E Motion; all our feelings need to be accepted and flow.

Regardless of how this situation was caused I want to explain how to recognise your own spaces and hollows inside you. I call these our personal **vacuums,** our emotional dents and weaknesses we all have inside. Be aware of them honour and understand them. Start listening to these inner dents. Once we acknowledge them, it helps to prevent the destructive paths they take; in other words, we learn to see the path but not necessarily walk down it.

Finally, the other elephant in the Mental Health arena is **nurture**.

For many experiencing trauma or severe mental health issues need initial gentleness and nurture.

Some Schools of thought suggest traumas in our lives can sometimes stop developmental at exactly the age the trauma happened. To throw blame anger and even abandonment at a person experiencing such extremes can sometimes be tragic.

Thanks to our 'survival brain' the **amygdala** and the **hippocampus** work together to survive immediate threats but **sometimes the hippocampus can recall events that are stored without any concept of time so a trigger from the past can upturn a tragic event that we may not even have realised affected us; PTSD has been linked to this process** (also see Chapter 9).

Once the brain has made up its mind that there is a threat it kicks off the physical body; our heart and our adrenals go on a rampage ready to fight the threat that chases us. **This is why anxiety is such a punishing physical process.**

Our 'time stretched busy stressful world' allows this process to be more viable for these awful mind states to occur. **It is not just a** case of 'get some rest' or 'do some exercise' as most people like to preach who have not experienced these frightening physical and mental reactions in our bodies; it is a chemical process that needs to be addressed in the right way.

Through understanding and acknowledgement, self-love amongst other methods in this book we can put the prefrontal part of our brain back in charge of the overactive child- like amygdala and hippocampus; it involves slowing down our lives sometimes and re nurturing ourselves within a safe environment and the right nutrition (chapter 9). Medication may null this process but the buried traumas still have to be dealt with. A really good description for adults and children of this process around the inner brain that I find useful is found here https://blissfulkids.com/mindfulness-and-the-brain-how-to-explain-it-to-children/

I have given a brief description of the amygdala and hippocampus so you know that these feelings are not just you, it is a chemical reaction in your brain. For some this is comfort and the link above can help you understand, it is also covered in Chapter 9 but you do not necessarily have to go into depth unless you want to. Each angle of tackling your condition and each chapter in this book should be adequate to help put the brain activities back in balance.

So, let's go to that child inside us all. *Even as I start to write these words I can feel the 'little girl' inside me worrying about the ridicule I may get if anyone reads this; before I would have worried with her; now I am able to reassure her that it's fine, there is nothing to lose here, I can write I can do this; "remember how strong you are; You walked through hell for nearly two years and here you are, it is so important for some that you share it. It is a message of hope."*

One of my 'fair weather friends' recently commented at a party after I told them I was writing a book to help people who were going through a tough time; 'I'll look forward to reading this book." I felt they were patronizing me.

Whether it is my shit or theirs, I can't help feeling that I need to prove myself and that because I fell apart some people still view me negatively or underestimate me. Some people still talk to me (in my opinion) with some pretend gentle empathy that instinctively makes me feel that they think I am a lesser human being than them because I fell apart. An 'agitated mess' that I reflect in my poetry, they ask: "How is your anxiety?" I never felt comfortable with this because it is not mine; it's a condition and I don't own it. I could be wrong in my perceptions and despite getting annoyed and getting a bit of healthy fire inside me, **I also know it doesn't matter now because my faith in me does not rely externally it is now within. This is a major shift.**

I have learned my worry about what people think is just an ego state that is irrelevant. I listen and acknowledge my ego **but do not let it become me**. It serves on a very superficial level. Deepak Chopra and Eckhart Tolle are great masters (amongst others) who can teach you, through their talks and meditation, not to take too much notice of the ego fed mind. I refer to them and others in Chapter 8.

I have found inner peace through breakdown to breakthrough so without much of an ego intent here it is; the words that you are meant to read that will help you move forward. If this book just helps one person change their life or recover then I am happy. If you are in this darkness now, **when you survive you will make a very interesting person with a lot of clarity gratitude and empathy**. This book is also a big salute to all you survivors out there. Try not to brush your experience under the carpet, honour it my friend; you are a true warrior.

When I awoke from this hell my perception of life was different, my regard for myself was different. So come on let's open up this dialogue and offer methods to help you and your loved ones move forward...but first a poem from my angst and about cutting through

these misconceptions and unwanted advice we often get fed to us during these times.

Cope

I know you can't cope Who could? Once Miss popular, always courting' Now a joke; Jibbering wreck begging, Exhausting.

You've read in a book the answer that I haven't read, So throw me a line, some advice from some column

It's exercise, it's mindfulness, it's getting over

This soul destroying solemn.

_{If only you had time}

You could Show me what to do.

'It's easy if you would just make an effort

How did you let this happen to you??'

```
I'm left to juggle Your words In
disgrace, I'm trying this method you
mentioned but can't put it in place.
```

Truth is I can't even function!

My head is so tight . My eyes stinging, I've not slept for a while. My tongue is dry and fizzy.

I wish you would have just held me but you are always So busy.

Rocking and Rubbing my hands In a heap. No one can help when you are in this deep!

The deeper I go the less people I see. My fear becomes fact; you have abandoned me.

Chapter 2

I get to recovery then fall in love; the rantings of vulnerability.

(warning: contains strong language)

When I realised that I would write a book about my experience of complete breakdown, these were my first raw words after a relapse following a relationship break up.

J broke my heart. God what a relief it is to say that! He may be a total wanker for whatever he did but he broke my heart.

I could go on about the unfairness of it all present the evidence and we would all conclude that 'yes that he was a total C***!'

However, you can't totally blame people for the way they make you feel.

I was vulnerable when I met him, and he knew that and you have to be some sort of a C*** to do that. If I had been on solid ground then I may have thought 'what a screwed up tosser' and moved on.

The truth is I've been following bad relationships patterns all my life and after having a breakdown I was able to break this. The shock was whilst just coming out of it I played the same hand again. I went for someone on their terms who was unavailable when I needed them. I wasn't yet recovered enough to realise this.Luckily, I had found a counsellor (in a long line of failed therapy) who would let me see this (thank you Andy).

Right now, my mind is running at a million miles an hour (it always did), but now I have to learn to sleep again and learn to rebuild who I am which is a very different picture to when I started this journey.

More to the point the real question here is "how can I help you?" This is why I have started to write with my spider scrawl across the page because I've realised **this impossible task is starting to look possible.**

For all the new Moms sitting with severe postnatal, all the men who feel rotten and frightened but feel they cannot (because of cultural gender constraints) burden anyone with their incredibly frightening state.

For anyone that can feel themselves falling apart now and all those who are breaking or who are broken: **hold the f... on.** You are children in the dark. Hug your frightened child inside because hope and recovery will find her.

All those people who don't have the time 'right now' as their life is just 'so hectic,' may offer you some useful advice they read in The Guardian about how to run a marathon to ease anxiety and then they'll fuck right off again.

My hope is you will find **the true warriors who are prepared to hold your hand** in the dark whilst you fathom how the fuck to get out of this terrifying daily existence. My wish is you can find a place where you feel safe where you are not alone to start a journey back to a different you.

My darling I want you to feel I am with you right now and this situation is temporary. I will keep saying to you to soothe you; ***This too shall pass!***

The truth is the unhelpful people can't really offer you the one thing that you really need. They wanted to think they had done their bit by lecturing or shoving some article in your face about links between exercise, anxiety, the benefits of mindfulness or some other wretched angle.

However, they couldn't offer you anything because sadly they had nothing to give. **You are disconnected, a social leper and are probably being told to take responsibility for this disturbing behaviour.**

'Don't let anxiety rule your life,'

'You got yourself into this mess now you need to get yourself out' (yawn yawn!!).

We can thank the ignorant for these unhelpful comments that plunge you more into despair, but at some moment in the future you will learn to forgive them for this is part of your journey.

'Forgive them for they know not what they do.'

I know what you are and I have been in your skin. You're a terrified little child in a very scary place. Getting out the house is a mammoth task right now; all you need is nurture but everyone is running away; I am giving you these words to shine a little light of hope on your dark path my angel.

Surviving each day in this state is brave enough commend yourself for that.

There may have been those you thought were best friends and maybe hopefully they are helping you or a top psychiatrist, a health co-ordinator, your own flesh and blood, but for all of them there were big barriers in front of them.

The first is their ability to cope. You are pressing their buttons. You are presenting to them something that is so threatening to them and their soul that they have to protect themselves; Fuck that hurts! They want to solve the mystery, tick the box, file you away, put a name on it; but you are an unsolvable, unpredictable, timeless exhausting mess and that my friend does not fit into our Western culture. You may as well try and stuff a fox down an ant hole.

Secondly; **the attempt to control it**. So, let's get this straight the meds may not be working right now they may kick in but this can take up to 3 weeks maybe 12 weeks maybe 6 months and hopefully they will work? If they don't you won't know your arse from your elbow because from hereon in we are playing Russian Roulette with chemicals. Meanwhile everyone is politely pushing you away; they're uncomfortable.

If you had cancer...they would be round your house at the drop of a hat, but you haven't got cancer. Your soul couldn't cope anymore...and **to add insult to injury the feelings of self-hate, shame, fear escalate your experience of abandonment by those who you would never have expected to abandon you.**

'You fucking idiot; you trust too much.' I think to myself. My Nan always used to say I trusted too much and she was right; in the depth of my despair I hear her chastise my vulnerability, my open heart and sensitivity to others that I was in denial about for years. I was the 'well liked voluptuous tall pretty party girl' and **now the skinny people repellent.**

'The breakdown that made me;' can you even think that this could be the case right now? Of course, you can't that is why I am typing because through these words in your darkness I want to show you light. *We can only shine light when there is darkness my friend.*

A tear rolls down my cheek a tear of pain rolling down my tense head. It feels like it has been squashed in a vice. I smack myself around the face for being the only person who got myself in this state or at least that's what everyone is telling me, and apparently that is what everyone is talking about so a friend told me "What the fuck has happened to Morag?"

I'll repeat that for you; you fall and you get "what the fuck has happened to Morag?"

'Sort yourself out, put some lipstick on, bake a cake!' So on and so forth, if only I knew getting out of anxiety was that easy (yawn) except yawning would be ace if I wasn't so fucking agitated; drowning while you watch, screaming while you cover your ears.

"Please God anybody. I am so sorry I did this to myself: Help me please show me how to get out!" My sobs and pleas remain unanswered.

Knowing who your true friends are when the shit hits the fan, may well be the first lesson you learn.

And here's the thing if you want to feel ANGRY -yes angry - because **the chances are you've spent all your life trying to appease, make people happy, helping everyone, keeping the peace**. You might have been the light and soul of the party? Too many texts not enough time to answer. Sound familiar? And here you are now **broken,** just broken and where are those C....?

Your phone is silent no longer vibrant with chirpy irritating little noises of expectant friends who long for your company; alone wriggling in agony on the bed then sat up by the radiator trying to stare out the window staring at a picture anything to stop this pain. It won't go away and no one cares to hold your hand and give you some hope.

 'No concentrate; must stay alive for my boy.' I grit my teeth head in hands; hands clasped tightly trying to swallow up and absorb the intensity inside this skull. Just get through each rotten terrifying second. My only release …. Cry and sob.

You may be lying on your bed staring at something for hours in desperate despair with no understanding of how to turn the button off, the button inside your head and the sickening feeling that churns from your solar plexus. The weight you lost the Brazil nuts you stuff down your face that took all your bravery to get from the supermarket; you managed three items but they will keep you alive, you go from a size 14 to size 8 in a matter of weeks.

And 5 feet fucking 10 inches tall and all people say is 'you look great." They've misunderstood something here and for sure they don't care if they misunderstood or not. They simply haven't got the time in their important life to offer you. Their time and nurture; to hold you and tell you it will be ok. That would help. However, 'hey you're skinny' and I guess that is a good sign in this crazy modern life.

If I didn't have a child, I would be dead by now but I have got a beautiful soul that desperately needs me so every second of torture I go through is inevitable, there is no choice, he needs me and he keeps me here.

I feel I will die anyway but if I write to him then he will know or he won't have the shame that I took my own life even though my mind continues throughout the day to look for ways to do this. I write letters just in case I lose control in this sleepless adrenalin fuelled state; I write letters to say goodbye.

Well baby child here is your hope THIS CAN ALL CHANGE!

Here's some other good news "Don't let anyone tell you it's your fault, *it is certainly not your fault ok!"* I want to put a big fat laughing emoji here. It certainly isn't your fault and yet the guilt slung in my fragile direction; endless guilt of taking responsibility for my state. Apparently I have the the power to change it now; how I am locking myself in my own suffering...bla de bla de bla. Thanks for these opinions but they are for your benefit and not mine.

Forgive yourself child, don't for one minute let any therapist (yes therapists), friend, family or professional tell you that it is your fault, **it is not.**

A mental health nurse shouts at me about my anxiety like I could curtail it and I'd 'brought it on myself,' like I could pop out of it at any moment. I was already terrified. Unprecedented untrained bullshit; be careful of your words professional people they can harm; the injured hang on to every one of them. Stay kind, stay compassionate and stop trying to egotistically throw your knowledge, but not experience on the vulnerable.

Ignore them all, all these destructive comments ignore them all.

Come back to this light that I show you. Let's get you out of this.

This may happen to any of those MFs that are feeding you this unhelpful shit right now. I know you don't want it to, you wouldn't wish this on anybody but it would be good for them to know their wretched comments can come from those in the mental health services themselves at all levels. They are about as helpful as an inflatable dartboard except you're the dartboard and they're throwing the darts right at you.

They're not here right now honey child and in your darkest hours, when the initial visits start closing and people realise it's not getting better, 'I'm out of here, she's wearing me out,' because you will be wearing them out; accept that.

The chances are you may find yourself alone and you will never have known such a terrifying loneliness and such a wretched existence.

They will then realise their modern schedules can no longer incorporate your breakdown so they will have to start throwing some blame at you......

'Look at the fucking state of you who on earth would want to be in a room with you; you are a vampire and energy sucker; get out of my house now.' I stumble out and drive head pounding I want to drive off a cliff but I can't because of the sweet soul who doesn't understand and the only person who wants me in his life right now is relying on me.

Luckily this time I have somewhere to go I drive to a caravan where a kind stranger has offered me his space; a kind stranger who selflessly offered me his safe corner for over a year and reassured me that his vision would come true; the vision of now. **The vision of recovery beyond any imagining.**

Now I am recovered honey child I will live and breathe hope back into you through these words. In that dark you will find diamonds underneath the layers of thick sorrow, diamonds you have never known and you will have learned to forgive yourself and not spend the rest of your life saying sorry. You will forgive those too that left; they were just scared like you; **they are not bad people at all**.

Before this breakdown 'sorry' was my favourite word. Now I am not sorry anymore; sorry for being me, sorry for being in your way. I'm not sorry anymore. I'm really not. Fuck all those 'sorrys.'

From leper to lover and loved, your path has begun; do not underestimate this journey you are on, you are a beautiful soul.

And so, you take the abuse; abuse for being ill and whilst one person shouts, another will take your hand and help you find your diamonds **because they do shine your diamonds; they will shine but you just can't see them yet.**

Those diamonds are your forgotten soul the little boy or girl you failed to hear or nurture for he has been upset for a long time. You will learn to love her and *genuine* people will then take seats in your life. That is such an important word because they are **genuinely** there for you.

These people or persons will know you; they will know your heart. They will not judge you. They are the magic when they come out of nowhere and bring your greatest gift at this moment; **Hope**.

You may never have met and associated with these people before this journey you took. Those who have suffered or know what it is to suffer. Those who have such insight and empathy that they will sit with you, clever enough not to suffer your sufferings but kind enough to understand your need for regular company and nurture beyond their own needs.

They will be able to drop some of their life and have the ability to understand and ask "How can I help you." and this will be the *'Breakdown that makes you.'*

These are rare gifts in a world today driven by screen realities and busy schedules in all the chaos they will stop and ask these questions "what can I do to help you? What can I do to get you through the next few hours? 'I may not understand always how you feel but I want to help you get through this."

"I can come over regularly on this day every..? Whenever you are feeling distressed you know where I am?"

They won't say; 'You need to do some exercise!" Meet me at this café! "don't let anxiety rule your life." I just can't cope with you.' They will just hold your hand in the darkness and ask what you need.

Your reply will probably be' I just want to feel safe and I know that someone is around.' Once you realise someone is there your road starts to recovery. For Indeed the first equation to your recovery is **Safety, Nurture, Connection, Structure (SNCS).**

A social media message after recovery

Lisa G; thanks for inspiring me to do this. You reminded me it was World Mental Health Day today.
I am Morag it is hard to write this but I feel it is important to share experiences and talk about mental health.
You probably see me on Social Media with a great life intact, but I am not afraid to tell you that for nearly two years I suffered severe anxiety and was sleepless and suicidal for a lot of those days.
I managed to survive it and hope this is a message of hope.
I am far from grateful that for whatever reason, this happened to me but feel because of it I am more insightful, perceptive, and self-loving than I ever was before.
I am writing a book called 'The Breakdown That Made Me ' to guide and give hope to both loved ones and sufferers through these dark times when our mental health jumps out of control.
Unfortunately for those who have to experience seeing their loved ones go through this please try not to;
Tell them they are responsible for their condition.
Tell them to go run a marathon it will cure it.
Get angry and frustrated with them.
Talk about them behind their backs.
Avoid them.

Do
Nurture; spend as much regular time as you can cope with in their environment where they feel safe!.Comfort them tell them it will pass...things change.
Be gentle it's not their fault.
If on meds make sure their meds are not making them worse.
Fight for a better mental health service and understanding.
Respect that they are fighting a phenomenal battle.
Thank you for all the angels who miraculously helped me ..xxxx
 and my son of course who is the reason I am still here.

> When I fade off into the darkness that you don't understand. I hope you wait for me to step back into the light. But if you choose not to, I'll thank you. Because if you never understand the dark side of me, you certainly aren't worthy of how beautiful my light is. My light is only for the ones who never left me alone in the dark.
>
> Stephanie Bennett-Henry

Chapter 3

<u>The story of how I got to breakdown.</u>

My first experience of severe mental almost from never experiencing debilitating mental health was after having my son. I was quite a late Mom at 39.

The birth was ok, I needed drugs that I hadn't planned including an epidural and, as my son was overdue, I had the birth induced. I am very sensitive to medication. Despite my Thyroid being screened as Normal I have a Goitre.

After the birth I bled heavily for twelve weeks; no one picked up on this and it was deemed ok. I was breast feeding and on the fourth month I came down with a fever for days. On the fifth day I went to the Doctors and was diagnosed with Pneumonia and given a strong antibiotic I had never had before.

Two days into taking this antibiotic I experienced very severe insomnia, something I had never had issues with. This went on for days, I thought I was going insane. It was terrifying.

Whilst going back and forth with my partner and my newborn baby to the out of hours emergency Doctors, most Doctors remained puzzled to my sudden demise. It was then on around the fourth visit an elderly Doctor asked which antibiotic (*) I had been put on?

My partner handed it to him and he put it in his pocket and said 'you're not having that back, unfortunately you have experienced a rare side effect from the antibiotic but you should make a recovery.' So rather unlucky you might say?

 *Antibiotic was Clarithromycin and usually new Mothers are more sensitive to medication than they would be normally. Although some studies do not always make a clear link (see below) more and more research suggests that a postpartum Mother who is given antibiotics or steroids up to 6 months after conception will be more vulnerable to Post Natal Depression.

https://pubmed.ncbi.nlm.nih.gov/30024041/

This higher risk makes sense when more and more studies show that our gut and brain system are linked (see chapter 9). Our postpartum bodies prioritising our baby's survival through our breast milk and when general fatigue kicks we may also be giving up some microbrial diversity in our gut.

A strong medication that literally steam rollers through these delicate microbrial and hormonal systems can rip up the balance in the body quite quickly during this time. Studies often mention this and the **thyroid** but they seem to focus more on the natural emotional and hormonal changes that happen after birth, rather than the medications our new Mom is putting into her body. (*)

(*) In the UK we have an 'adverse reaction' reporting system known as 'The Yellow Card scheme.' Ask 10 people and the chances are not one knows this system. Many studies point to the fact that adverse reactions are often not reported and cover between 1 to 10% of the true figures. https://www.researchgate.net/profile/Neil-Miller-7

These flaws in our medical system does not allow us to see patterns and understand that many individuals do not respond as they should to medication prescribed. We also need to ask if a system such as this would find it advantageous to have such reactions reported with great efficiency...urm; I don't think so! As far back as 2004 The Yellow Card System was described as fatally flawed in the BMJ and very little has been invested to improve it, https://www.bmj.com/rapid-response/2011/10/30/fatally-flawed-yellow-card-scheme

Following my experience both factors (in my opinion) are just as significant, yet judging from the lack of studies the side effects of these major drugs too often are not reported. Mine wouldn't have been either if it were it not for the experienced Doctor (backed up by the Psychiatrist after) who discovered it.
https://www.ncbi.nlm.nih.gov/pmc/articles/PMC5659274/

My advice though is this; **If you are a postpartum woman/ new Mother with her baby DO NOT take antibiotics or steroids unless they are absolutely essential to keep you alive.**

In fact if you are run down or vulnerable for any reason then unless it is life- threatening I would suggest antibiotics can exasperate the condition rather than heal it.

It turned out the pneumonia I had was viral following bloods and an X ray that came after the damage was done. The Doctor at the time was taking precautions (as he should) to a potentially life-threatening disease, so there is no blame.

Perhaps in hindsight, I would have insisted on the test results being rushed before taking the antibiotic.

The Post Natal Depression lasted for around three months but I had the support of my partner at the time and a daily visit from the mental health team as I was a new Mother.

They put me on a Benzodiazepine (Lorazepam) and an Antidepressant (Sertraline). After recovering I came off these quite easily. It was unbeknown to me at the time that the Benzodiazepines can be highly addictive. (see notes below*)

The second episode of poor mental health for me was triggered off in January 2015 after my partner and I split up. I seemed fine. I then developed a physical condition in the gall bladder that wore me down for a couple of months.

I lost a lot of weight during this time and no one really had an explanation for this other than I may have had a gall bladder infection. During this process I also reluctantly took two courses of antibiotics; one for the GB infection and one for a chest infection a month later (December 15). I was utterly fatigued during this illness and started to feel worried and low as I am very much an active person.

Whatever happened by February 2015 I stopped sleeping I had also started taking small amounts Lorazepam intermittently, I had found in the draw from my Post Natal Depression. This was not a good idea; whether it was the chicken or the egg either way I was spiralling fast and losing weight rapidly. My fear deep inside was that I was dying.

As I write this it becomes so apparent to me how the physical and mental body are so intertwined. Rundown, get ill, take antibiotics wipe out your Serotonin, start to worry...spiral, spiral. Already vulnerable systems from Post Natal antibiotic and stress of being a single Mom, guilt around toddler, living in an unfinished building site of a house. There is always a pattern to these events.

The medical profession started the process of giving me antidepressants which became a countdown; some said they would hit in two weeks, others said six weeks, some said three months. I think at one point I was told 6 months by this time I was virtually chewing my hand off with anxiety and didn't know if the meds were exasperating it.

Either way they didn't kick in and the Sertraline (which I had taken for PND) had a reputation for high suicide ideation rates (particularly with young people). Although, many medical institutions will deny this, the links are out there to be read. The untold stories as well as the poorly and rarely reported side effects are the pointers we use to assess the safety of these procedures. Sometimes it is just NOT YOU that is the reason for your mental downfall. Bear with me on this for there is no judgement on whether you take medication; I just want them to be the right ones!

https://www.ncbi.nlm.nih.gov/pmc/articles/PMC3353604/

https://www.drugwatch.com/ssri/suicide/

When I complained of suicidal thoughts the Doctors said it was my own anxiety **and upped the meds**. Upping the meds made things worse with the Sertraline, it felt like there was train tracks running through my head and my head felt like it was between a vice; I became heavily reliant on the Lorazepam by this point. The

Doctors seemed to be happy that I would be ok on Lorazepam as I had taken it before for PND and had come off it with no ill effects. This was not to be the case this time round.

As well as a pressured feeling in my head, not allowing me to think straight and the train tracks running through it for most of the two years, I suffered with severe headaches and insomnia. Sylvia Plath describes this feeling in her classic, but incredibly tragic book 'The Bell Jar.'

I really don't want to try to prove to you how hard this was but I am recounting some of the toughest memories and feelings of this utter mess that became my life.

I am doing this so you can see how bad it is and yet how good it became and to make others understand how easy it is to misunderstand and make the situation worse.

I stood on the edge of a metaphorical cliff everyday whilst in this calamity; this breakdown that was happening to me. A suicidal insomniac looking for some peace, but as much as I tried, I couldn't get out of the physical and mental hell I was in.

So, if right now you're having trouble with your sleep just remember I survived two years of pretty much no or poor sleep. Try and trust that your body is an amazing survival tool that will find its way back to recovery. Try to find some peace in these words.

I also have read now A Rose to A Sick Friend (Tessa Goldhawk) a hypnotherapist who helped me and has an extraordinary view on illness. Her book is about acceptance of illness but Tessa also understands the great strain mental illness has on our bodies.

"When you are ill there is no good anyone telling you to be sensible, or to pull together. Though you might agree with them

intellectually, nothing can counter the blind horror and fear you feel when you are suddenly caught up in pain and illness...

Let me say straight away; you are not being punished. This is a common feeling that it is completely unjust or unfair that it should happen to you. Both these reactions are OK, but neither of them are accurate."

Many creative acts are born of pain. Getting to know and love ourselves will only come through pain."

For me though the most comprehensive simple phrase that those who were prepared to share my awful company was this;

"This too shall pass."

I spent a lot of my time in anguish trying to get people over as I was terrified in this state on my own. Exercise was many people's recommendation I would try so hard to do this even though it felt so frightening. Once I bought a bike and biked eighteen miles, on return I collapsed in my house and sobbed; I was exhausted and trapped.

I live in a beautiful place and I would stagger to the beach in a thick red coat that I always wore. One of my friend's husband once cruelly mocked me 'Here she comes in her red coat" he had a nickname for me which I can't recollect. In this state I just wore whatever was in front of me and the coat was thick and warm a protection for my skinny terrified body; it reminded me of **Leonard Cohen's 'Famous Blue Raincoat'** a lost misunderstood vulnerability.

People felt uncomfortable with me, so mocking me would make them feel comfortable because they didn't know how to deal with my energy; it drained them. I just wanted to get through the day.

I'm not even sure how I managed to get dressed my brain just did not work, the basic tasks became impossible.

I knew and had decided I was going to die anyway I could not survive like this hardly eating, thin and not sleeping. I wanted release and it was better to kill myself and plan it so I could write to everyone; I thought that might provide some clarity for people rather than having to watch me rot away slowly.

In these states there seems no end to the suffering so taking that decision to end it somehow felt responsible and perhaps a relief for everyone else whom my presence became intolerable.

One very important person would creep in to the fruition of these plans; **my son** aged 5, who knew I was not well but wanted to be with me and like children their souls are so pure. Whilst everyone else had given up on me he remained a true soldier who was anxious when he was not with me because he knew something was wrong.

As normal I would try and act in front of my son; sometimes I would sit and sob: it seemed the only relief I had. I know this was not ideal and sometimes, even though he can't remember that his Mom had a 'poorly brain,' if I cry now (on rare occasions) he gets anxious and I think this is a trigger for him. So, I talk it through with him and tell him it is important for everyone to cry.

My ex Mother in Law, Jan, kindly came to live with me for a while; she bought some little sharp knives for cooking. These became a daily fantasy of how I would use them to relieve the anguish I was in.

To stab all three of them deeply in my chest would be quick and efficient. I had written suicide notes; I was way ahead of the severe guidelines for suicide risk, but there were no facilities available to house me, I was not at a critical level apparently. The cruel system of government cuts had lost me as it had many.

So here I was with a plan but where would I do it? Who would find me; how it would be? Then one scenario would play over in my head.

A teacher walks into a class and asks for the beautiful blonde boy in the corner, the one that had become a bit withdrawn and shy; unsure of himself (who is now brimming with confidence BTW) to come with them.

This teacher was trained to tell children tragic news; the news was that Mommy had died; he would later find out that I had chosen to. This would play throughout his whole life and his personal suicide risk would increase significantly. The sadness and horror of this forced me to hold on for dear life and hope to God I would live to tell the tale; **I did and I am.**

I was looking after my son 50/50 after about three months. A lot of people especially friends with children weren't around. The notion that I wanted to take my own life appalled people. They went white they couldn't cope; being in my presence was ghastly. I was a social leper. I felt I needed to tell people but learned it was not the right thing to do if I wanted people to visit me.

At this point I wanted to say having a child was the best thing that ever happened to me. I absolutely adored my son. I am a good Mother but in this state I cared so much that I didn't want him to continually see me suffer with an ending I had come to believe would be tragic.

As I have said I wanted to relieve everyone from my presence in this world. I looked after my son but there would be times when I would just cry. The feelings and physical symptoms I was experiencing were so severe I couldn't hold them back or hide and children are incredibly perceptive anyway! One psychiatrist told me it was ok to cry in front of him, another that it wasn't. **Conflicting views were rife within the service and this left me feeling unheard, unsafe and disconnected.**

I would put out texts to friends I had known asking if anyone was around as being in company made it easier. There were a handful of beautiful people that would sometimes offer time knowing it would be difficult but still went out of their way.

A lot of people were unavailable it was very convenient for them to have another schedule. What I was really saying was 'help me please, I am struggling to look after my son. (*) A lot were busy with family stuff. I knew how toxic I was, I felt disgusted with myself that no one would want to hang out with me but in my body I was getting through one black second to the next with little or no relief in the form of sleep or escape; there was no escape

(*) I love the modern lyrics of Shawn Mendes 'In My Blood'. I heard this the other day it made me feel quite emotional it does describe some of the pain I felt in a beautiful heartfelt song.

My poor son; I was pushing away his friends, I'd gone from a social magnet to a repulsive energy vampire. My hate for myself and the situation I had been told by many 'I had got myself into' sometimes would project into me picking my skin and often out of sight I would slap myself hard around the face and sob.

I got texts from some frustrated friends telling me to **'sort this out; I could not let anxiety rule my life.'** I cannot tell you how destructive and unhelpful comments are when you are in these high states of anxiety. Even some professionals would reiterate the lines 'You got yourself into this now you need to get yourself out." It felt like they were angry with me. I had enough negative emotions and problems to resolve, but in my head being despised and abandoned made everything so much more difficult and intense.

If I had the key, I would have opened the prison door but it was nowhere in sight, nor was the jail keeper. It was a single solitary high security cell of pain and as much as I stared at each brick and the heavy metal door there was no possible escape at this time so I couldn't figure out how I had got myself there and why people would tell this to me?

People who say these sort of things to those who are suffering or who **say 'suicide is a selfish act' do not have understanding of the pain in anxiety and depression.** It is this language and attitudes towards mental health that we need to transform to a more accepting and nurturing place, so we can offer more support in this field. It *is for this reason I gained the passion to write this book. If only to have the misunderstood and unheard, understood and heard.*

I remember opening the curtains in the summer to the sunshine. I hated it. It meant another day to get through. I would either ring loads of people to try and call for some solace, or plan a routine to try and keep my son busy praying for the day to end.

Once my son was in bed I would shut my eyes but nothing settled a bright glow of alertness would ring round my head. I was in a war zone and my head just wouldn't shut down. Knowing that this was not just my natural anxiety and may be chemicals in my head made it even more frightening. At least with no chemicals the body eventually just passes out; with unnatural processed chemicals the body cannot always take its natural path.

I had some friends who tried their hardest to accommodate me but this was not a task to be taken on by one or two people. In this society we don't have to take on responsibility for others' mental health. If it's our family it can be different but everyone had their own issues and to take on a case this severe was too distressing so one by one they turned away. Some close friends never even showed up.

This still haunts me now. To be abandoned was terrifying. Thank god I had my son and that stop memory of fucking up his whole life because now I have never had such a great life.

Now, my son and I laugh and joke sometimes with each other. He is such a sensitive confident, extroverted both physically and mentally healthy and I feel so privileged to have the task to teach him wisdom, humour and kindness in this world.

I truly believe I have something to offer whereas before I felt 'unworthy' of people. I was a pleaser; now I invest in myself not in a selfish way but more of a believing way.

Every day now I am grateful and everyday this experience has made the joys of life so much more beautiful and sharper. **These words are** *the hope I give to you my friend.*

Now let's talk about the subjects you need to talk about; how to recover. There is also a simple foundation everyone needs to start the process of recovery and perhaps if some of the people I knew had this guidance they may have been able to have offered something without feeling overwhelmed.

SAFETY, NURTURE, CONNECTION AND STRUCTURE (SNCS)

My Beautiful Boy. (2015)

My beautiful boy

With slightly chubby curious hands.

So loved, so loving!

I thought I would want to be strict

When you were in my tummy.

but now I think 'Have tantrums, be alive!'

Let me hear your giggles

And see what you find so funny.

Kicking up feet in the air

Pretending to be 'little hare'

"Guess how much I love you Mommy?"

'Not as much as I love you little hare

Head full of longing and despair

For my angel, my hands have been tied

When I watch your beautiful soul smile.

I have never felt such love.

And I have lost time

In this vile prison of despair.

A tiger in a cage

Full of sedative not knowing how to behave.

Watching her cub being so brave.

Chapter 4

Medication: will you or won't you?

(There is no Judgement in this chapter at all, just information you need to know.)

Let's deal with the medication first; it's a very important part of the mental health difficulties you have found yourself in. If you're having a breakdown then the chances are you're a sensitive soul which means you might be very sensitive to meds too. They may either provide you with a partially functioning platform of normality to start moving your life in a positive direction OR they will set your little dinghy into a treacherous storm worse than the unknown waters you were floating on before.

Taking medication (or not) should be seen as a very important decision **that another person in your life is monitoring with you.** Don't just rely on the Psychiatrists or Doctors as sadly right now (2021) the mental health service in the UK do not have the resources to fully monitor you.

Also remember the main solution a psychiatrist or your GP will offer after their assessment will be **medication**. Not only are there some very powerful natural alternatives with less side effects there are also methods and environments that can all lead to healing. The choice is yours, but I want you to know what you need to consider when choosing pharmaceuticals as a choice to help with your recovery.

Medication is such a complicated subject. I am not telling you whether to take medication or not. I can tell you though that if you hit the wrong medication for mental health they are simply dangerous. **If you're having to take them to survive it is ok** for now but what got you here can be relearned or changed and medication can sometimes cover or sabotage this process.

If you are on these medications now it's ok but just make sure you know how to come off them as the doctors and psychiatrists often misadvise on this. As someone who is highly sensitive to medication, I learned the hard way.

This chapter will provide insight on taking medication, and if you choose, coming off it in a safer way giving you the best possible chance of no withdrawal or side effects.

If medication works, it can simply give you a break from the head torture of mental illness to start getting your life back together. The main medication for anxiety and depression are antidepressants.

Benzodiazepines and Zopiclone should be avoided as a last resort; they are incredibly addictive and produce side effects that exaggerate the symptoms you took them for in the first place; **there is the irony of some modern medicine practices. They do not cure, they just mask temporarily and then exasperate the initial imbalance.**

Remember in the last chapter it was discussed how adverse reactions are under reported, so the full understanding of the effectiveness of mental health medications are not understood so it is important for you to get this right.

I want to run over my experience briefly to show that the wrong medication can be devastating for you and your family and sometimes you don't realise that your symptoms are worse because of the medication prescribed and not because of your health.

My account of this is a 'mish mash' of chaos whilst sometimes good friends would try and fathom out my arse from my elbow and what drug was doing what, no one in the medical field was monitoring it. I was in a trap where the psychiatrist had instructed the mental health workers 'not to discuss medication' as it was not the issue apparently; my past, potential PTSD and my anxiety was.

In Dr D's (my psychiatrist at the time) 'patronising' opinion I was getting 'obsessed with the meds.' Inside my body the meds felt like they were doing a lot of damage, I was still not sleeping and was suicidal. How could they be working if I still felt this way, **wasn't the point of them to make me feel better?** I wanted to discuss the meds because I was crying out in pain to be heard; desperately needing a change.

These professional people were not in my body; I knew the medication I was taking was inflaming my condition but I felt no-one was listening.

I will go as far to say, without any doubt, some of these drugs I took are responsible for lives lost in and out of the mental health arena. Some of the anti-psychotics, anti- anxiety and anti-depressants pharmaceuticals are prescribed for pain yet when people stop taking them unbeknown to them, they can cause extreme withdrawals; anything from irritability to insomnia to suicide ideation, to guess what… suicide.

I am not going to spend time simply sharing studies with you. I will direct you to one, but once you start to research you will understand that taking this medication should be a well considered decision. If you can't concentrate during this time then ask your friends or carers to do so some research on your behalf. you.https://www.pharmaceutical-journal.com/news-and-analysis/news/antidepressants-associated-with-increased-risk-of-suicidal-thoughts-in

I understand however that when you are desperate you will want relief and eventually when I found an anti- depressant that gave me relief I really was grateful. However, they are not designed as long term drugs and generally the recommendations are 6 to 12 months.

However, with mental health sky rocketing and NHS resources decreasing, it is often for the convenience of the system to stay suspended on these drugs for years. I say suspended in a sense that you forget who you were and just remain on a chemical platform where you can cope too scared to change anything.

My take on this is there is simply not the resources for patients to come off them and receive less invasive treatments. Secondly people mistake withdrawal symptoms as their own anxiety. As a result, they race to get back on the meds; too frightened to experience the withdrawals that often accompany them. At the same time convincing themselves that their mental illness is incureable.

There are two types of anti-depressants: **SSRI's and SNRI's**. The differences between them is explained in the link below. They are both designed to change the balance of Serotonin, a neurotransmitter in the brain, so it is more available in more needed areas. Serotonin regulates mood and sleep. (https://www.drugs.com/medical-answers/difference-between-ssris-snris-3504539/).

For me it was an SNRI that worked eventually after having two SSRI's which produced hideous side effects. What these websites don't always say is that they **ARE** addictive so you cannot just stop taking them and expect your brain to go back to normal without experience powerful reactions whilst it adjusts to get back to its 'normal' balance. Coming off them should be a well-planned slow process; a method that I describe in this chapter.

For some, anti-depressants can give users **personality changes** and cases have come to light of people taking these medications who became unrecognisable to their loved ones.

In 2012 a tragic case in Colorado, U.S came world news (there will be many others)....when a young man, studying at university at the time, dressed as batman, with no history of violence machine gunned down and killed 12 people in a cinema.

Even though he is still in prison his increasingly anti-social behaviour before this horrific crime correlated directly with the psychiatrist's choice to **increase his newly prescribed** anti-depressant. He wrote a diary and the change from normal anxiety to delusional was quite apparent; again in direct correlation with the prescribed SSRI and its increase.

His family are still fighting the case. Although extreme, this shows that personality changes can be one of the side effects of anti-depressants. Lethargy, head fog and weight gain are also more common side effects. https://www.bbc.co.uk/news/resources/idt-sh/aurora_shooting

The above case alone (and there are others) should be an indication that those prescribing these drugs hold responsibility to intensely monitor and assess their patient. Not so long ago, this would have been one of the roles and the community hospitals for mental health, that have in many towns been closed, would have helped to assess.

How often do people go to the Doctors feeling 'low' and come back with a prescription for an SSRI or an SNRI with no further instruction except an appointment in a few weeks' time?

There are then the **'tranquilizer'** family of the Benzos that Doctors do state are highly addictive and should not be taken for more than a two-week period, otherwise the body becomes dependent and the withdrawals are way worse than the original complaint; imagine that! (The Benzodiazepines are the 'pams'; Lorazepam, Diazepam etc.)

Doctors are less reluctant to prescribe Benzodiazepines (Benzos) because of their recent links to Alzheimer's and Dementia. Benzos would be used more for the severe cases like mine and tend to give quick more instant relief whereas an anti-depressant can take up to 12 weeks to kick in and sometimes that journey can be difficult especially if at the end the drug has not complied.

Once we have become dependent on Benzodiazepines or other tranquilizing /hypnosedatives acting drugs such as Zopiclone for sleep or mental relief, coming off them has often severe withdrawal affects. Benzodiazepines have been likened to coming off heroin or cocaine and sometimes worse as I discovered.

A Doctor and Psychiatrist may give you a programme over weeks to come off these if you become addicted but the reality is it can take months so again withdrawal should be a carefully planned process depending on your sensitivity.

My advice would be to ask organisations that deal directly with drug addictions such as Addaction. Once you get to a lower level follow my method at the end of this chapter find a method that will work for you. https://www.rehabs.com/pro-talk/getting-your-brain-back-together-after-benzo-withdrawal/

One thing is clear; most people who have come off Benzodiazepines feel that if they are offered them again they will refuse point blank. So do not take them above the short- term recommendations or simply do not take them if you can find other less harmful methods. I know this is easier said than done though.

Monitoring and being an advocate of someone having a breakdown all comes back to time, kindness and understanding. I would like to think anyone reading this book who is close to the sufferer is able to offer a regular time slot and whilst doing so monitor any changes in medication or behaviour.

So, after I describe my experience of pharmaceuticals, at the end of this chapter I'm going to tell you some basic guidelines to follow, to help you distinguish between the drug reaction and your own. This is from my experience but also research the links that I have given you or let the people who are supporting you do some research.

Question: If you are going to give a drug that changes someone's behaviour should they be monitored?

The answer to this is YES, Yes and Yes, absolutely, and every Doctor who gives out anti-depressants should be responsible with their practice for the outcome of that patient. This is not necessarily the Doctor's fault, as you know our NHS is under so much pressure especially now that we live in a world whose medical systems focus more on profit than people.

A sick person is worth more than a well or dead person! Do you need me to get you literature for that? I don't think so, but we can take some responsibility in this by questioning and delving behind the medical facts and experiences of patients. You will find encyclopaedias of people harmed and silenced by modern pharmaceutical drug companies. Open your eyes and books and research. No drugs company is going to risk their demise by openly sharing this information as their prime objective is monetary success.

This is not to say that doctors don't care, most go into this profession because they want to care, but they are put into a system where their time is stretched and a holistic approach to patient care is limited.

Too many professionals working in the medical field have a time limitation with people; ticking boxes and spending time 'covering their ass,' takes real time away from the patient.

Reaching targets has come to dominate the whole working system, but this does not work for people with mental health issues as their sense of time is very different.

Would it surprise you to hear that the people on the highest tier of the mental health ladder were some of the people who made the most misinformed and potentially fatal decisions about my mental health treatment.

My initial problem with anxiety came from a physical problem. When I stopped sleeping with the uncomfortable sensation in the gall bladder, I noticed my anxiety had increased. I had never felt this level of anxiety except for after having my son when I got PND (previously discussed).

So just to reiterate I got through my initial Post Natal Depression in 2011 which occurred four months after having my son triggered by an antibiotic. I was given a Benzodiazepine called Lorazepam that calms your nerves; and it did. I was also given an antidepressant called Sertraline. I had my partner at home at this time and a daily visit from the mental health team.

This second episode and ultimately the breakdown was different; my partner had left me, I was living in half a building site and trying to look after my son. Admittedly, when I couldn't sleep I had occasionally used Lorazepam that I had found in the drawer from my postnatal depressant three years before; When I became anxious the doctor (who wasn't my regular doctor) had prescribed the same meds, Lorazepam and Sertraline; it made sense I guess?

This time the effects of the Sertraline were very different. My poor sleep became no sleep. I became more agitated. My head felt like there was a steam train in it continually (this has been described by others taking this drug). When I took the Lorazepam at night time I could feel a fight happening in my head, suddenly the steam train would stop then I would be knocked out. I would sleep for two hours then wake up with the steam train banging in my head in terror...it was torture. I was not in control of my head. It's hard to explain how frightening this feels.

The doctors did not monitor this prescription I was given and I left to my own devices. Sertraline is an interesting drug and has worked for some people. It is often given for PND because it has been tested in trials on Mothers who are breast feeding and is deemed as safe.

As one of the cheaper anti- depressant drugs it is prescribed regularly and especially to teenagers. Some studies have suggested that it has caused higher suicide and suicide ideation in

teenagers than other antidepressants within its field.
https://www.nhs.uk/news/mental-health/antidepressants-linked-to-suicide-and-aggression-in-teens/

In my previous fields of employment, I have worked alongside young people which I loved. The thought of young people dive bombing further into poor mental health after taking medication to try and help them breaks my heart. Their trust in the medical system makes me think that they would conclude that their declining mental health is them and not a bad reaction from the drug prescribed.

Remember in Chapter one I wrote briefly about the **amygdala** and **hippocampus** parts of our brain that react to trauma in order to survive. Sometimes they get the wrong signals or time frame and an event can remind or trigger a traumatic event stored from the past; **the hippocampus is sending the amygdala a trauma response but cannot distinguish the time frame that the stored trauma happened in, hence initiating a short or long term anxious response commonly described as PTSD or Post Traumatic Stress Disorder.**

A need to be re programme the brain or visit the trauma in a different way is a potential solution; it is an intricate process that involves some time and care by looking at experiences and traumas that have been buried. **Rapid eye movement (REM), hypnotherapy and NLP (Neuro Linguistic Programming) are some of the therapies that take this approach.**

Focusing on self-worth and how these experiences have affected the victim in this way is another possibility. **Again, this is retelling and reframing a traumatic story so the victim can cope and rebuild who they are and my 'vacuums method' in chapter 7 follows this approach.** Although learning about our vacuums, I believe, is a healthy exercise for anybody. It is an awareness and forgiveness of all the chinks in our armour we have which make up our wonderful imperfections.

All these approaches can be a more successful long-term solution than a medication that creates game changing chemical responses in the brain. However, If an anti depressant works it can be helpful in the short term or even for relapses but the issue is whether they will work effectively.

So, if someone commits suicide after taking an antidepressant or indeed coming off one: the chances are it won't be put down to the drug but the person's mental state.

So now imagine how many untold statistics are out there from death by pharmaceuticals; many people are still fighting in big court cases over this and many big pharmaceuticals have the ability to silence people with cash. Whilst medicine has its place, its original ethic to help people has become hindered by a need to protect profits.

Within the mental health arena, the pharmaceuticals rely on the fact the person was already depressed when they committed suicide; it was just a symptom or development of their condition.

So back to my medical journey; this time round on Sertraline my condition became worse, I was informed that it would be better to wait as things often got worse before getting better at first they said three weeks then I was told up to three months, then six months. **I was in mental agony**. I managed two months on it.

When I went into the doctors in a highly agitated state, around a month or so on Sertraline, the young locum told me she had got advice and I was to be told that **these agonising train tracks in my head were not an unwanted side effect from the meds but it was my own anxiety**. They concluded it would be better to **increase the dose**. Now go back to earlier in this chapter Batman who gunned down 12 people; his psychiatrist increased his dose when his symptoms became worse. If you do increase the dose SOMEBODY needs to monitor; luckily for me I wasn't experiencing mass personality changes just more extreme insomnia and anxiety.

The dose was then increased and quite soon after I thought my head was going to explode.

Patients who are put on new mind-altering drugs/ antidepressants particularly are supposed to be under weekly reviews. **This simply did not happen.**

During this time, I was also taken off Lorazepam as it had been deemed I'd been on it for too long. Honestly I think they had forgotten then looked up my notes; over two weeks Benzodiazepine can become fatally addictive.

Everything got worse and worse, my brother came down to stay and was horrified at my state.

I finally got to see a psychiatrist urgently on a cancellation. The doctor, by this point after two months of Sertraline, took me off it.

I was put on a new anti-depressant, Mirtazapine, and was given Lorazepam by the first psychiatrist (Dr D.) I had not got addicted to it during Post Natal Depression so I could be put on it now. At this particular meeting, I had packed my bags begging someone put me into hospital but alas I was not a severe enough case as most of those hospitals have now been closed or sold off.

Dr D described my state at this point as not 'being able to string a sentence together.' She used this as a platform later to cite my improvements as you will read.

My brother took me back to Devon for a while at the beginning of the breakdown and the sleepless nights continued. Occasional relief from Lorazepam which I was well and truly addicted to by now would override the insomnia and the horrific headaches I was getting.

I returned home and over the next few months battled every second of life in a horrific state. A friend of the family (Mike) came to stay at my home and Jan my (ex Mother in law) both tried to take it in turn so I was not alone. I was terrified of being alone even with my own son. There seemed to be no answer on the horizon to whether I would ever see my 'normal' life ever again.

I had been deemed ok to look after my son but I was distressed that he would see me in such a state. I also had issues of him waking to find me dead. This was from a childhood trauma I had suffered which you will find in Chapter 6 'my jigsaw.'

Everything was coming back to haunt me; although **now I feel my fall was my salvation, which I couldn't have even imagined in my wildest dreams back then when I was in so much pain!**

After my operation to remove my gall bladder which I had originally complained about before the second bout of extreme anxiety I had hoped to get some relief from the anxiety as I had convinced myself that the weight loss and general feeling rubbish followed by anxiety was caused by the gall bladder issues. The reality was very different.

It is hard to imagine now lying there recovering from a general anaesthetic whilst my head would not shut down. It was torture, my head was more alert in some mental torture than before the operation.

Despite lack of sleep and intense anxiety my gall bladder op scars healed; from this I learned how resilient our bodies are.

Mike would come over and stay and take me out for walks. Skinny and wretched, I was grateful for his company; thank you Michael and Jan for this period; just having someone in the house made me feel safe.

At this time, I was on a mixture of Zopiclone and Lorazepam to get me some sleep which would knock me out for short periods of time, and in the background an anti-depressant that was supposed to be coming to fruition and get me some sleep and respite from the terror I felt; but sadly never did.

What I will say is that when I was finally given an anti-depressant that did work it relieved my head in a matter of hours. Proof in itself of how ultrasensitive I was in my reactions to chemicals.

I was grateful for this relief but I don't want to say it was my salvation as I don't want anyone to think that medication is their first port of call. If it is, **waiting up to 6 months in mental agony for a drug to start working and getting addicted to Zopiclone and Benzodiazepines in the process is certainly not a route I would recommend!** (I want to put a laughing emoji here because even reading this sorry chemical mess seems ludicrous; so much so it is laughable.)

I was then put on a regime to come off Lorazepam as funnily enough it can cause severe anxiety! The psychiatrist, Dr D, had given me a prescription for Diazepam to come off the Lorazepam it was over a two week period. When I finally came off it, I hit severe agitation. It was a waiting game I was told it clears your system in two weeks.

After two weeks I was still in a state I was told by the Doctor **that clearly this was not the drug but my own anxiety.**

The truth is it was difficult to tell my arse from my elbow now. I just wanted to slip away and stop the pain. I just wanted relief from it all but I had my son, and I just couldn't let him suffer that loss.

The sentence the doctor said sent shivers down me. **He told me that after a year of suffering this was my anxiety and not withdrawals** from the Benzodiazepine. **Misinformation like this can cost lives.**

In other words, there was no option than to continue with this severe agitation and anxiety with a hope it may go but it was all self-inflicted. **This was simply not true.**

This is one of the most dangerous misunderstandings and communications about a drug that has been readily prescribed.

I am sure they had their place and may have helped me **but even though they are physically out of your system for two weeks the effects on your nervous system can last for months. If you are on Benzodiazepines then keep reading. I got off them and you will too my friend.**

It is well documented that people take months even years to get off The Benzodiazepine family. *Their withdrawal effects are likened to heroin and cocaine. Some say the withdrawal is more extreme. Some never get off the drug. Some never live to tell the tale.*

Can you start to feel the misunderstanding and mistakes that were being made here?

A psychiatrist has a text book definition description of a Benzodiazepine withdrawal. It doesn't work for me but I am made to believe that what I am left with is this eternal severe anxiety which has now not gone away when more than likely it was a common side effect of a drug that paralyses your central nervous system and creates long term withdrawals. [Benzo Withdrawal: Why I Ignored Medical Advice and Listened to the Internet - Benzodiazepine Information Coalition (benzoinfo.com)](benzoinfo.com) Example given is one of many.

Go to an Addaction worker and ask about Benzodiazepine withdrawals; go to a GP/psychiatrist and **under their NICE guidance the information is totally different.**

Imagine trying to fathom this out whilst in severe agitation or even worse, imagine not discovering that the anxiety you are experiencing is 100 fold because it is a drug withdrawal; Off the cliff you go, 'another preventable suicide.' Here is a suicide caused from misinformation and a pharmaceutical.

The same goes for antidepressants, perhaps not as harsh as the benzodiazepine family, according to some doctors and psychiatrists you can just come off antidepressants (Dr D told me this in one of our sessions), or you are given a very conservative withdrawal period. **This simply is not true for many people.**

1.You come off them and start feeling anxious, back to the Doctor you go. You are told 'this is your anxiety' back on the antidepressants you go for the rest of your life, too scared to come off them, too scared to trust your own healing abilities. Any recovery and improvement has been sabotaged by anxiety induced withdrawals.

2.Or you sink into a depression as you don't want to have to go back on brain altering chemicals as you haven't felt yourself for years and off you go to the cliff.

Anti-depressants can also have withdrawals and depending on each individual will be affected differently. We are all made in a different chemical mould, and unfortunately the medical profession does not always account for this.

I found a safe method to come off the antidepressant I was on; after the first time, over a 6 -month period I fell into anxiety again. Yes, even six months was not long enough. I had come off it too quickly.

I took advice from a herbal practitioner and I also substituted my days without meds with CBD capsules; it took me two years; the same amount of time I had been on them. I have put the method at the end of this chapter if you want to try it.

I will say I have had a couple of relapses where I had to take the anti depressant which is in my cupboard. This can happen so don't beat yourself up about it but do take smaller doses for shorter times then you can come off it over a shorter time by making tiny cuts.

My view is that it is not forever these blips are memories or PTSD responses particularly if you have had an acute episode. I do not want to be on pharmaceuticals and this is my choice and I will continually strive and explore natural options. The pharmaceutical that works is for emergencies only; but it has to work and be useful to you.

What I will say about CBD though is you need the right dose and quality is important so ask people who use it for advice.

I now use Holy Basil as this amazing herb can lower Cortisol levels and if taken long term can significantly reduce anxiety. Holy Basil Anxiety Benefits and Dosage (superfoods-scientific-research.com)

Both CBD and Holy Basil are covered in the Nutrition chapter.

At this point I want to say this is not necessarily advice for people who have had to take medication all their lives but if you have had a nervous breakdown then when you are truly ready to come off the antidepressants of course inform your GP, start reducing slowly; everyone is an individual when it comes to drugs some can get away with just coming off them; for a lot of us who are sensitive this is not the way. **A lot of people who experience breakdown are likely to be highly sensitive**. Either way it is not worth taking the risk.

I want to thank Frazer at this point as well as Jan and Mike who were my support team because they got me through this… but it was during this time I met Simon. Mike, Jan and Frazer had all taken turns in living with me but they had to move on they couldn't be with me 24/7 and Frazer was still around but not in the house. I'm not sure how I would have got through this first year without them.

Simon is a healer; he saved my life. During my stay with Simon when I didn't have my son (see friends) …when Jan, Mike and Frazer had moved on with life and I really thought I was alone I was taken by an old friend Kirsty who appeared out of the woodwork. She drove me to visit Simon.

Kirsty I am so grateful for this part of this next part of this journey that emerged.

Simon is a well- known healer in the St Agnes area of Cornwall; he has helped many. It would still take another year to recover but regardless of healing Simon offered me a safe place to be when I didn't have my son. During my time with Simon, I made a decision to come off the Mirtazapine; I was still feeling rotten. The psychiatrist, Dr D, who had already miscalculated my Benzodiazepine withdrawal, did not want to take me off Mirtazapine. I had been on it for a few months, I had major headaches was suicidal and still not sleeping. She said if I wanted to come off it it was my decision **but she recommended I stay on it.**

I asked her if she would try any other antidepressants as by this point I was desperate; another psychiatrist had mentioned one called Venlafaxine (SNRI). As stated earlier it was another group of the anti-depressant family.

Dr D would not put me on this as it was an 'upper' not suitable for me she thought. There was no medical option for me now. This was another miscalculation on her behalf as later this was found to be the drug that settled my anxiety within a matter of hours.

Dr D had a vague plan to try me on Chlozopine; a drug widely used for Schizophrenia, a seriously heavy drug; that I knew because some of my severe mental health clients I had come across in my job were on it. A dangerous route leading to a life lost on heavy drugs; **almost a worse scenario from when I started my journey with anxiety.**

I remember her revealing this to me on the phone and a shudder ran through me. I knew I would never let anyone get me to take this heavy chemical with high sensitivity to meds. How could she have got this so wrong? From living by the sea with my son to flying over the Cuckoo's Nest with no return.

Despite feeling suicidal, Dr D had reported I was getting on with life. I was managing a few hours of work a week but I was still in a living in hell. I had taken six months off work in my part time job but was keeping my foot in the door after six months so I didn't lose my full pay and then my home.

Everything was so close to just falling away from me with a risk of losing my home, my job in very quick succession. My manager at the time, Sarah, showed me so much compassion and patience and thanks to her I still have a job. Even 5 hours a week was terrifying but somehow I got through it. I made up the other hours when I was well enough.

Remember this was a local council job so the sick pay offered was excellent. I was lucky enough not to be on a zero hour contract and can totally understand how people become homeless very quickly when their mental health declines. Help with any benefit applications and offers of food may be a necessity to get people through these awful periods.

Dr D's letters always reported improvement but I was not feeling improvement. The lack of sleep and thudding headaches were still destroying me. I would cry and tell her how much of a problem these were and asked if she could prescribe a different medication. She would refuse perhaps I was a lost cause now and she had given up on further options for. In her letters she mentioned these as an 'after thought' (see the poem after this chapter 'The Battles Outside My Head') at the end she added "she complains of headaches and **some** lack of sleep."

Her letters reported improvement. I am not a person who wanted to stay in this by any means. I am not a natural 'victim' but making these false positives I felt was dangerous. I wondered whether these letters were about her agenda and not my recovery? Sometimes I would read her summary letters and through my head fog would wonder who this person was she was talking about.

When I would call the Doctors asking for something different the Doctor would call Dr D who after only seeing me for 30 minutes every month would quote the same sentence back to the Doctor who would repeat it to me *"Compared to how she was when she first came in when she could hardly string a sentence together; she has made massive improvement,'* There would be no compromise or movement from her position and there I was still in hell, rocking and agitated.

I felt like I was in the bottom of a pit about to be covered with earth people could see me and I was shouting for help but they were throwing dirt on me and walking away.

As I said earlier, through research and experience, despite not being as damaging and addictive as Benzodiazepine, **you cannot just come off an antidepressant.** The effects are not as often as harsh as a Benzodiazepine but your symptoms can become worse. More importantly the withdrawals can surface sometimes three to six months after stopping the medication if you have come off them too quickly. All this is confusing for someone who is mentally aggravated.

I am telling you this so you know how careful you have to be with doctors and psychiatrists, if you are taking these drugs. The lack of funding and the misunderstanding about mental health and individual response to medication makes the current situation in our mental health support system sadly lacking.

A good society shows its strengths by the way it treats its most vulnerable and here we are throwing bread crumbs at the mentally vulnerable from behind a wall of bureaucracy, austerity and an 'I'm alright jack' mentality.

Again, I want to reiterate I am not pointing my finger here; there are different aspects to everyone's situation. That is why I am writing about each separately. **Please be a good advocate for someone who is suffering if you can.** I found a lot of people have already judged and don't listen to the voices of those suffering seriously.

At this point I had learned how to carry such pain but knew I would not be able to carry it forever. **Of course, I thought it was forever because it feels so eternal. Having reassurance and love / acceptance around and people saying 'this will pass,' was paramount in the end and helped me hold on.**

Dr D's recommendations and treatment were not working whilst she was writing that they were. As much as I tried to explain she could not understand how it was to be in my body and my need for different medication. Her status and knowledge blocked my cries for help.

My light at the time was Simon, who I have mentioned. I was practically living in his caravan when I didn't have my son. I had explained to Dr D that I would have to make the decision to come off the Mirtazapine Simon backed me up Dr D said this would me my choice and if I wished I could just come off it **which as I said before is simply not true**. Can we afford to have untruths when working with people who are so delicate?

Initially when I tried to come straight off Mirtazapine, as she had suggested, I got even more agitated pacing and pacing, my joints became tender and aching and my gums felt they were shrinking in my head I was on my own in the house it was terrifying. I was horrified to see on the internet others going through similar difficulties which helped me feel I wasn't mad. **Remember I hadn't been warned about any of these effects.**

With Simon's support I came off it slowly and painfully and with extreme withdrawals; I took about three months but, as it was not helping me, I just wanted to be off it ASAP.

A friend of mine during this time took me back to the Doctors and asked again for benzodiazepine to calm the effects as I was experiencing extreme agitation again. The Doctor in desperation prescribed Diazepam again and I believe this cushioned the side effects of the Mirtazapine.

What a dichotomy I was in! I was slowly unravelling the mess, every foot forward there were five back; remember my sleep was shocking I still felt there was no way out. **I had been ill for over a year.**

I slowly came off the Mirtazapine often staying at my good friend Simon's place. I would just lay there in an agitated heap. Sometimes I would call Samaritans, new counsellors. I was forever searching for answers. Sometimes I would pace and Simon would sit and just be with me while keeping me safe.

Dr D was totally on the wrong path with me; can you imagine how many people get wrongly diagnosed and placed on a chemical hell journey trusting the decisions that have been made for them and then blaming themselves. **Remember that the health profession is not in your body so you must make it clear with the help of an advocate how you feel and any changes that take place once medication is prescribed.**

This truly terrifies me and is one of the reasons that I think the medical side of poor mental health is paramount to get right, not only as a way forward but as a safe way out if the sufferer chooses. ALL the options and knowledge should be put before them including non-medical. **Why are we still working within a limited system that only serves one industry and can cause potentially more harm?**

During this time friends and even family would call me or text to tell me off offering simplistic solutions such as 'let go of the past'…'do not let anxiety rule your life.' These statements just seemed irrelevant; I couldn't even focus on the past let alone let go of it!

Once off the Mirtazapine, I began to lower the Diazepam so slowly shaving tiny bits off the tablets it was an impossible task and took months.

I was still experiencing mostly sleepless nights.

I had a new Mental Health Worker for fortnightly visits but they were often cancelled due to work overload. **She did one good action; I was assigned Helen, a** lady who would visit weekly and take me to exercise classes and a great art place down in St. Just. I dreaded going and had so many preconceptions of the people I would be hanging out with. Once there I met people who had gone through nervous breakdowns and were actually lovely to talk to.

I was so afraid to be put in a box that stated 'I was severely mentally ill.' My perceptions of being mentally ill as I grew up were people to laugh at, people that weren't accepted in society. I was desperately trying to hide these stigmas for fear my son would be made fun of if it was obvious to people that his Mom was 'mad,' 'mentally ill,' 'a looney tune.' **How wrong as a society we have got this and how much healing we have prevented from locking people in lonely stereotype boxes.**

Helen (I only know her first name) but how grateful I was that she came in my life. I have yet to thank her but hope one day she might read this book and realise how important people like her are in this system. She changed the course of events though her genuine concern and love and yet is on one of the lowest pay tiers.

When she first met me, she came into my house and I told her my story, when I looked up, she was crying. From this moment I knew I was safe with her. We both cried together hand in hand. She remembered when she had her hysterectomy out and felt emotionless; no love for anyone even her son. **It was like she could feel my pain and there it was empathy and suddenly I felt safe.**

I felt safe enough to go to exercise classes, and an art project in St Just, as long as she was around, I could venture into a 'normal life.'

As well as feeling safe with her Helen would reassure me that this would all pass. She had seen others like me that got better. These words were all I had to cling onto. I still felt like I was clinging desperately onto a life that I did not want to be in.

One day Helen could see that I was still distressed; she commented that this was not good enough...She thought I should see a psychiatrist again at which I just cried. She suggested I see a different psychiatrist this time.

In one phone call (Helen who knew the Secretaries; some who just didn't understand urgency she thought), **She cut through a three month waiting list and got me an appointment with a new psychiatrist the next day before he went on holiday.**

I went to see him with an old friend (*) Colin another beautiful soul who had also popped his head out of the woodwork and shown true kindness as well as housing me many times. He took me to this appointment.

(*)A text from a safe friend at the beginning of the book was Colin's message to me.

I had written notes for the psychiatrist about my life and how it was the sleeplessness, the suicidal thoughts, the agitation that were torturing me daily.

Rather than writing how I had been improving in his assessment **he wrote the truth.** I looked *'dishevelled, thin and tired.'* He agreed that I must come off the Diazepam and gave me a reasonable withdrawal 'knowing your sensitivity to drugs.' I was already cutting this drug slowly anyway.

He put me on a micro dose of a drug called Quetiapine used in large doses for schizophrenia but non addictive, he also prescribed Zopiclone (as addictive as The Benzos) which I agreed with my doctor not to take. Finally, an anti-depressant called Venlafaxine.

The Quetiapine got me some sleep (even though I had a hangover feeling/ thick head in the morning this was a tiny effect compared to what I had endured; insomnia is torture!)

The Venlafaxine, which I sat for hours before taking in Simon's caravan, strangely **worked immediately;** my head stopped feeling compressed.

The dose of Venlafaxine was increased over the month as I kept dipping, it just made me feel normal again. Feeling normal was a beautiful/ strange feeling I had forgotten. I had so much gratitude and clarity knowing that this drug had shifted some chemical imbalance in my head and had got me on track.

My friend Frazer, another warrior of kindness, a man that had such empathy and understanding and had stayed with me at times had watched me suffer and had just offered his time and kindness and utter patience. I met Frazer shortly after taking the Venlafaxine and saw immediately that I was close to myself, the Emma he knew and remembered nearly two years ago. **He started to cry.** I had never seen my friend Frazer cry before. That feeling of joy that had come back that feeling of life we often don't value was at last with me again. **I looked at Frazer and suddenly realised how he had suffered so much along with others watching me through all of this.**

This drug was the trigger for me to get my life back. A couple of psychiatrist and occupational health professionals had suggested this drug whilst the psychiatrist, Dr D, I had at the time was away. I had been reluctant but after a while I had been so desperate, I asked to try it. Dr D had refused; **this may have saved months of suffering.**

I was able to get off the Diazepam and I was working alongside Addaction now. My first worker hadn't offered me anything other than treating me like a junkie; you will recognise this experience in my poem 'The Worker.' I felt that there are so many gems in the mental health profession that really 'get it.' There are also those who don't and **it is tragic that people with mental health issues get unempathetic responses from workers as this only worsens their state and makes them believe more so that it is all their fault.**

I managed to change my Addaction worker and I will say Addaction as an organisation are great as they have more realistic understanding of addiction and individual responses. My new worker, Agnes, was a great support during the beginning of my recovery.

Everything was falling in place. I had taken the initiative to go on a website (spare room .com) and ask for someone to help round the house after one bad choice I had found a lovely woman called Denise to take up this role in return for free rent. She was like an over- zealous Mother which is what I needed; as well as Simon, here was the second figure that had filled the **'nurture'** part of the equation. Admittedly she talked a lot and still does, and is a dear friend to me.

Denise's chatter in the morning would be hard when I had my Quetiapine head but I was overjoyed to be living back in my house with her Motherly presence for both me and my son, because of course my son would have felt my fear and now we had a safe maternal presence in the house. I cannot tell you how comforting that was and how kind Denise was going way beyond what I had asked.

If I was worried about sleep, she would help me make a decision whether to take the Quetiapine or not. Denise is one of those people in life who was born to care; born to make people feel safe.

I had also met two friends at School; single mothers Laurian and Marie who had both been through rough times, we became a team available to each other 24/7 and still are, these people are priceless gems .

I am also proud that I survived and ever grateful that my friends I have are available and supportive of whatever I do. When I had a relapse two years ago, after coming off Venlafaxine too quickly, my concentration went. Laurian, who is a teacher, came over and made me stop, made me a cup of tea then helped me tackle daily routine step by step with her full support. None of them showed me once that they would reject or abandon me; totally the opposite. This became a healthy platform to recover; chemically stabilised and feeling safe and connected. Here were my requirements for recovery **safety, nurture, connection and structure.**

From this I want to show that 'Yes' the right drug did turn the tables but can you see how unmonitored I was and how many drugs it took to get the right one. I did need medication but part of the effects was covering the negative effects from the other medication; add to this my original anxiety and there are many layers that created a perfect storm for a mental health disaster.

Try not to get into this mess and follow the simple guide below. **There are other options and as you read through this book I hope you will find your light.**

Please also note that a drug that suited me may not be for you. Venlafaxine helped lift me into some normality which some of the other drugs had exasperated but some people find Venlafaxine creates sweats and their head feels like it will blow off. The point is I know it works for me.

Many anti-depressants cause brain fog and weight gain. So, despite the five minute consultation when that prescription is produced, make sure that it is the right choice for you. Take it seriously and place people in your life if possible to monitor you or if you are a carer or friend place yourself in that person's life regularly if you can to keep an eye on them.

I have always been into natural medicine so being like this was so hard. It was everything I was not. I never imagined in my worst nightmare that I would turn into a 'pharma junky' desperately trying to pop pills to ease the internal hell I was experiencing. I also never imagined that from being so popular I found myself a repulsive energy vampire that few wanted to be in sight of. The brave ones gave me their unconditional support not knowing how long I would remain in this agony. It was because of their support that I had the courage to climb out of the hole I was in.

Now I do not want to be on pharmaceuticals all the time. For my job as a Healthy Lifestyle Advisor (oh the irony) I advise people coming into my clinics that have been on drugs for years and years; anti-anxiety, anti-depressants, even though they are still depressed and anxious! High blood pressure tablets, painkillers, laxatives to combat the side effect of constipation and stomach lining; pharmaceuticals to repair the suffering stomach from all the chemicals it is trying to digest...and then there is the liver.

Many Doctors have limited understanding of nutrition and although some conditions start with a suggestion to change diet many outcomes are a medication.

We are over-chemicalised as a nation even **young women** are highly encouraged to take hormones to protect them from pregnancies. The agenda is simply keeping pregnancy lower but what is not recognised is that hormonal changes can cause poor mental health. Here is a young person's account of being given the 'implant' as a contraceptive measure and the response she got when it went wrong.

"The Doctors and Nurses arranged very quickly for me to get an implant in my arm as a birth control.

Even after it was put in, I felt tearful. Over the next few months my mental health declined, I lost my confidence and my relationship with my boyfriend became worse. I had stopped going out and my school grades had dropped.

I was also losing a lot of blood during my periods. These were all noticeable after having the implant.

One night I became so distressed I found myself wondering in traffic wanting it all to end.

I spoke to some people about this, I was scared. They told me to immediately call the Doctors.

I did this the next day and asked them to take it out. **They were reluctant to do this saying I would have to get someone at the contraception clinic to do it. They tried to make out it wasn't the injection. They wanted to treat me with iron tablets for the heavy bleeding and anti- depressants for the mental issues.**

After a couple of weeks, the clinic finally agreed to take it out. They insisted I went on an oral pill, I didn't really want to go on the oral pill but they were very persuasive.

I can honestly say though that the minute they took that thing out of my arm I felt relief and back to normal. How could they have been so keen to put it in but not take it out when I begged them to. I felt let down." (T age 16)

With more pressure from social media young women are hormone injected, fully waxed ready to serve young men's high demands that are pushed into their brains on social media: not (in my opinion) the basis for a healthy society. *If we do not teach young women that chemical changes in their body can affect their mental health then we are not educating them. T's example above shows that instead of dealing with the route of the problem causing depression and anaemia, they would rather that she had iron tablets and anti-depressants to cover the problem.*

This is insane. Now if she gets a side effect she won't know whether it is the implant or the anti -depressant and if she comes off either she could get withdrawals. **She went to that clinic with a perfectly young balanced functional body. She now has several problems; can you see the madness in this? The pharmaceuticals have made her ill at what expense?** To prevent a pregnancy? There must be another way? **This is how we treat our young people so imagine the regular prescriptions dished out to adults.**

Sadly, pharmaceuticals do not heal or cure a symptom they mask or hide it. **The pharmaceuticals are interested in the long term sick because this is where they make their money.**

Natural medicine is also very powerful and can have side effects (some good) but the aim and objective is to heal; not numb or stop the effect the body is displaying. **Behind every physical condition will be a journey that got that person to this place.** What we call 'Alternative' medicines such as Acupuncture, Herbalism, Chiropractors aim to look at that journey and repair the damage with an objective to sustain the good health achieved.

Antidepressants may be necessary and helpful sometimes but getting the right one, for some, is like Russian Roulette. I was in such a state that it was hard to make any major decisions about meds but somehow I found my way out of this crazy maze and am mostly free of these drugs now.

For more information see the information section at the end.

The Mental Health system is a frightening place because it is under resourced dangerous and misinformed. I discovered ignorant people working in it who lacked compassion and empathy. This can be confusing and frightening for those with a mental health issue. There are also of course some total gems and I am so grateful I found them.

Unless it is life threatening you can look at other alternatives there are very powerful ways you can help your mental and physical health. If you need to take something don't beat yourself up, but try to avoid the Benzodiazepine family and Zopiclone as these are highly addictive and take months to get off with side effects worse than the original complaint. **Only ever take them for short periods if you have to.**

So here is a basic meds guideif you feel you have to take pharmaceuticals during a breakdown or relapse.

1.**Avoid Benzodiazepines and Zopiclone**; if you have to take them do so with absolute caution for no longer than two weeks.

2.**Try one drug at a time,** if possible, otherwise you will not know which drug is giving you unwanted side effects. A better option to an immediate fix is an antidepressant/anxiety but it can take two or three attempts before you get the one to suit your chemistry.

3. One of the most common ones are the SSR's; Citalopram, Sertraline, Fluoxetine, Mirtazapine; The one I eventually took is in a different category SNRIs was Venlafaxine. As an alternative you can try CBD oil, Holy Basil and/or St John's Wort as just a few examples of a more natural approach with less, if any, side effects. The GP or medical practitioner will assess how severe your symptoms are.

4. Yes, it can take up to 6 months for an antidepressant to work but if you get **so bad that it is unbearable into the second month then come off it and try another one.**

5.**Make sure you book regular appointments with your doctor and make sure someone is monitoring you if you are taking antidepressants; these are brain altering chemicals that can give you relief to start rebuilding your life.** However, they can also throw you further into the pain you are already experiencing and **it is important that you or others around you can identify unwanted side effects.**

6. Not sleeping is awful but try not to be so desperate that you will take anything to stop the torture. **Your natural body will eventually kick in and put you out.** If the chemicals you are taking make sleep worse, then the natural body is more limited to kick in.

6. **Feeling safe and having company are important whether you are taking drugs or not.**

7. Once a chemical has started working positively put gentle exercise and nutrition into your daily routine. This is your platform to get better then once you feel strong enough you can reduce **very** slowly. **It is not a rush take your time and generally you should take as long to get off the antidepressants as you have been taking them.**

8. **Set up a weekly timetable** so you know what you're doing and when. Try and get helpers and carers to volunteer a regular small amount of time with you each week for different activities (see Chapter 4a.)

The Coming Off Method That Worked For Me (in collaboration with Tim S my herbalist);

Ok so say you have been taking an antidepressant or benzodiazepines and **you are now ready to come off them** and I mean really ready; don't rush and try to come off too early if they have helped you...

Maximum time (reduce this according to the amount of time you have been on it...the 30 months may be necessary for Benzodiazepines for example.

- Reduce the regular dose by half over a period of 2 to 3 months, longer if needed. Once down to the lowest dose;
- TAKE ONE DOSE OUT PER WEEK FOR 3 MONTHS THEN;
- TWO DOSES OUT FOR THREE MONTHS; you are now on 5 out of 7 a week.
- THEN THREE DOSES OUT FOR THREE MONTHS now 4 doses that out of 7 days.
- Continue to 3 doses a week **then half one of the doses for 3 months.**
- Half one of the other doses for three months and do that with each whole dose.
- **Now on 3 half doses a week take one out;** you guessed it for 3 months till you get to NO doses.

- This can mean the total time to come off it is 30 months and, if you start to feel side effects, you can delay the next stage till your body has settled.
- **N.B when you get to 3 doses a week some people like to halve them and spread over the week; 6 doses over 7 days then start reducing in the normal way.**
- If you are feeling confident or have only been on the drug for only a few months you can change the period of adjustment from 3 months to 1 month for example.
- With Benzodiazepines you may have to **literally start shaving each half** then doing one month then shave 2 tiny slices off again for the next month.
- **If you feel really anxious try to go with it.** This may last for a couple of days whilst your body is getting used to the new dose, but **if it is unbearable take the dose up again to the last time you adjusted** and stay on it for a bit longer.
- It is all about letting your body adjust to these chemical changes. **You may get away with coming off it in accordance with NICE guidance alongside your doctor's advice** but if this is not successful, then try this slower method.
- the bad effects may simply be withdrawals and not you.
- Remember '*slowly, slowly, catch a monkey;*' be patient and if you feel you get to a lower dose and become wobbly then stay on that dose.
- If you feel you have to return again to using meds once you have come off them; **don't worry you haven't failed** but just **go on a very low dose for a month.** During this time, you will feel a rollercoaster of feeling ok then feeling anxious. **Try let your body adjust but don't immediately increase unless you feel desperate.** The outcome will be that you can stabilise on a lower dose than you have previously had.
- Go back on it with a view that **it is not forever.**
- There are other methods available but this one worked for me. Good Luck.

I am taking **CBD capsules** as a replacement for the anti-depressant for a few months and Holy Basil; research these alternatives, but always remember it may not suit you, everything is individual and even natural meds can have side effects so, if possible, get a loved one or carer to help with this. **CBD cannot be taken with Benzodiazepines,** so always check with your health professional first. Just like anti-depressants, natural meds don't work straight away so take them regularly and be patient to see results.

Here are some alternative natural methods to implement to help with recovery and during breakdown if possible! Firstly, though, when looking at these here is some good news...

1. *Change your mind set;* Don't get too hooked on 'bad genetics' in your family (see Evolve The Brain' and Deepak Chopra talks on the microbiome. (The Microbiome: How to Talk to Your 2 Million Genes – The Chopra Foundation) Out of millions of Genes only around 25000 are given to us by our parents; we are 95% microbiome so nurturing and helping this system with good diet can be a game changer for physical and mental health. Bad life can trigger bad genetics but we are also capable of changing this process again. By reading others dramatic stories of recovery, it fills your brain with positive patterns to help with recovery. Go to Nutrition and my chapter on spiritual approaches (chapter8), including medication. These may be really helpful angles for you.
2. **Repair The Gut** (see chapter 9 Nutrition); there are so many links with poor mental health and gut bacteria, a life time of poor diet or alcohol can damage the gut causing Leaky Gut Syndrome. The gut has been compared to the brain and known to hold in it large amounts of Serotonin (a feel good chemical.) Repair takes a simple routine for a few

weeks of natural based food. So, you don't have to be a saint but for a while make some positive changes then keep some of the habits within that daily routine.

3. *Cannabodoil. (CBD oil)* derivative of the hemp plant but expensive at the moment, has been used to help with Alzheimers getting people off multiple pharmaceuticals. It has cured some cancers and stopped depression and anxiety. Healthline.com have some facts but facebook groups are also on the rise and can help share information.
Always do your research. I take the capsules as the oil can get a bit globby; good quality and fairly affordable capsules come from www.LoveCBDoil.com and Holland and Barrett. You may need a higher purer dose. Doctors are quite familiar with CBD so always best to inform your doctor if you want to take this whilst coming off your meds.

4. St John's Wort can be a powerful calmer and can be taken with Passion Flower, this is a gentle approach for mild anxiety and depression but some people swear by it as a strong substitute for pharmaceuticals. It can be obtained on prescription in some parts of Europe. St John's Wort can also help **menopausal symptoms and I would also recommend Red Clover, Starflower oil and Evening Primrose for menopause as well. These can be taken together.**

5. *Holy Basil* is a phenomenal herb; go to nutrition and look at its benefits. CBD has had a bit of reluctance from certain research as reacting to Benzodiazepines for example. It appears that Holy

Basil does not interact with meds and is a highly revered favourite in Asian countries.
6. *Kombucha*, again back to the gut, a miraculous culture you can prepare and grow at home producing a health tonic. It increases gut bacteria and is good for a vast range of serious health problems including depression and cancer.
7. *Keffir*; same as above but a culture that grows in milk, again cheap and easy to produce.
8. *Glyconutrents*; see my Nutrition pages. Sometimes pure **exhaustion or chronic fatigue** can cause depression and the three additional plant based substances I would consider for this are **Reishi Mushrooms, Lion's Mane** and a powder supplement called **Ambrotose by a company called Mannatech.** Go to Chapter 9 for more details
9. *Exercise*; Yes when I was severe, exercise wasn't good, I was exhausted but as you get better incorporate physical things into your activity. I bought a dog much to the joy of my son when I was starting to improve, this gets me out every day and resets my head.
10. *It is exciting that new research is finding alternative drugs/ plants to treat mental health and even PTSD.* **Ketamine infusions and Psilocybin (from magic mushrooms) are being used in 'micro doses'** and the results are looking good. Keep your eyes peeled for these and look at A world without antidepressants: the new alternatives to prescription pills (telegraph.co.uk) and watch the amazing film **'Fantastic Fungi'** on Netflix. This is not just 'Magic Mushrooms' but Fungi themselves have many healing properties as I mention the use of Reishi and Lion's Mane in this book. The fact is that over a decade before the American government banned the research

into Psychedelics such as Psilocybin for medicinal purposes in the 1960s, it was seen as a very serious and promising outcome to cure serious mental health conditions. Although still illegal there are a lot of studies to show the great benefits to mental well being of this amazing organism. The underground mycelium networks Fungi provide are not only fascinating but magical in providing a symbiotic telecommunication system by which trees link to each other in order to pick up pathogens and communicate to their fellow trees and their off springs...yes communicate to their off springs! Watching Fantastic Fungi is a 'feel good' experience within itself. So let's keep our fingers crossed for more development in this area. **Don't forget these are Micro doses; taking Psilcybin or Ketamine recreationally is not a good idea if your mental health is fragile right now; just keep watching for new research.**

11. *Time*; *SLOW* your day down. Try and find room to be kind to other humans; we have just forgotten how to do this in this 'dog eat dog world.' **When you are well try slowing your time down at home; this is a very healthy thing to do it makes you enjoy and put in more quality to the present.** We have lost this ability in the culture we have created. We feel we have got to tick so many things off and this is why mindfulness has suddenly become so popular. It is a simple skill that we have untrained our busy brains to do. Just to be in the **now** is what mindfulness or 'presence' as Eckhart Tolle likes to say, is about. We have very different brains at the moment as the outcome of being glued to a screen all day; effects of which are still unknown. What we do know is that mental health issues are rapidly increasing significantly and

trying to slow down our movements can in turn slow the brain and reduce stress levels.
12. **Intermittent fasting** can help with anxiety and re setting the gut. (see Nutrition, chapter 9).
13. **Other herbs known to help with anxiety/depression**; Ashgwanda (also helpful for sleep and thyroid), Valerian; helps to cure mild insomnia, Lavender oil to relax.
14. **Incorporate at least 5 veg** into your diet every day and less processed food; make soups; put fat such as coconut fat and drizzle olive oil onto salads whilst reducing sugar content. Read 'The Microbiome Solution' (chapter 9 see books at the end) she has great recipes in the back and it is a real eye opener to how meds and over use of antibiotics can affect the gut.
15. **Reading or podcasts** that calm me; Neil Donald Walsh author of Conversations with God' said 'When everything changes change everything'. Eckhart Tolle and Deepak Chopra also see reading recommendations in the back of this book. Brooke Castillo 'The Life Coach', Byron Katy.
16. **Remember this is a journey,** there will be a few roller coasters here: recover from a breakdown will see you in life from a new positive angle... hold on you are a brave soul.

Following a chapter on meds I present a poem about meds and other attitudes that make poor mental health even harder to get through.

The Battles Outside Of My Head

The shame; I am writing this Because sometimes I still feel shame. And so small if not shame. I feel anger. Like somehow, I was to blame.

Pretending your ok after being screwed over; I'd love to go back to the way we were. but left to Discover alone. I pretend, when you ask 'How I am? And '<u>my</u> 'anxiety?' Like it is something

I fucking own!

The being heard; I would like to have known Medication Running Train tracks in My head Splitting in 2 (better option To be out cold dead) Was actually The wrong one; But alone Unmonitored

And 'nuts'

 it was all my fault a decision Like this Funnily…was difficult!

Despite their Calm collective Glances at me and years of study. Let's' learn to listen' persona. Let's understand. where was the empathy?

(Not any part of your Degree?)

The box tickers; I was broken And u were breaking me more. Leaving me unchecked. As long those boxes were ticked when I walked out that door.

on our bi monthly swaray, your 20 minutes assessment of me, while I begged for your help stated I was doing ok! My brain felt like it was being devoured by snakes; a foot note in letter;'occasionally she complains of headaches!'

The Pharma gamble; Let's play then..

Pharma Russian roulette. 3 months of unknowing in the unknown Unmonitored in hell; the table is set! Head spinning heart thumping addicted and hooked 'it's not working this!' blocked were my scream. And chemically fucked

You're the most agitated person I've ever seen let's get you off the Benzos and on Mirtazipine; Oh no that might be a benzo withdrawal or perhaps not; this is quite bad let's try stretching your head on Amitriptyline and dose you up on a bit of Pre Gab. We have beta blockers they may calm you down but you're on your own to experiment because there's no mental hospitals in town. I know you're oversensitive to these and sometimes you turn yellow but most people we get on these after a while feel mellow.

The only message and plan for me so it seemed. was failing this I'll stuff her with Clozapine. No turning back from that one. a life surely gone. a serious chemical a bad trip to be on.

Bon voyage!

The ones too busy and too frightened; You could walk away from the body I didn't want to be in. I was a prisoner of its confines but it pressed those buttons and was stealing your time

There is too much bravery in too many kinds and this is also about your health 'At the end of the day you've got to protect yourself.'

Over privileged and over protected; what were you supposed to do.? your thoughts straining the notion this could happen to you!

However there is a solution an offering you could give ..wait for it…Drum roll………………………………*you could offer advice!*

(oh Joy!) Here it comes…

'I should learn to be alone'

'Only I had the answers"\'

'Any more?'..oh yes luckily you had tonnes!'

('Please that would suffice;

oh no you hadn't finished…ok if you must

and always say it twice!')

'Look what you have become…'

'U got yourself into this!

U need to get yourself out!'

'Come on! Throw some more at me before you run!

And more good news; despite all the stress I had caused to everyone, you were happy to stay in touch. It has been hard for you seeing me in disgrace so your amazing assistance will be by text or phone.

But not face to face!

The model of support is not based on hope. but more on offering bad advice when you think you can cope.

Fear of being with me; So I curled up And fought the inner war. On my bed at home

Retarded brain default of error. No good to anyone; constantly In terror

No more Miss Popular now. A Self-inflicting Self-hating. Sickening

Unstable agitated cretin. Thinking of friends. Sitting round betting

That I had not got myself out of this silly mess I got myself into .I wash my hands of her. life is too short/ My hours too few!

Frightened Mom. I didn't end up with that knife in my chest the scene I played over and over. for my own release

and everyone else's peace

Cause I thought that would be best

 I held on for my son even though most could not make space for this dysfunctional case

Cause I was a humiliation/A social leper/An emotional vampire

That would never get better.

Don't feel bad; Most didn't have the kindness or the time when it got rough. You did nothing wrong Just chose a social blindness When u had enough. There was no room for me In the lives I thought there should be).

The hope bringers; There was a glimpse! A few souls Held my hand in the darkness

And stroked my damaged head and softly spoken.

"my angel this will pass, You will be fine, there is no shame you are just a bit broken."

Sail Through this treacherous sea" and I will sail with you Into sunshine..

Until this is just a bad memory. u had faith. It was just temporary

It is just temporary.

And in the dark I learned to see. A tiny spark. A beginning

Of recovery

(to the handful of people that saved my life thank you)

Honest, true and biased; an anger poem. I had to get off my chest for all the miserable advice I got when I just needed time, hugs and connection, but of course this is my angst. I don't have the other side of the story but my advice is if you can't offer time and kindness don't feel that text messages and long phone lectures are helpful...just don't do it. As for professionals, there are genuine beautiful people working in the system but some have been worn down with box ticking and others are just that; box tickers. The true people who were able to help were extraordinary and empathic ...that's not to say others who weren't able to help were bad, just too locked in a system of limited time.

Chapter 4a

FIRST AID FOR BREAKDOWN (A GUIDE FOR CARERS)

Equation; Safety +Nurture +Connection + Structure=Recovery S+N+C+S=R

SAFETY

1. **Keep yourself safe by setting time limits and boundaries;** start asking other close friends or family what they can offer weekly?

2. Person **needs a roof over their head...** may need help to sort out/apply sick pay/ new benefits if they were working; **they must know that for now they don't have to worry about work.**

3. They may need support **looking after their dependents/children.** Make a plan that involves contact otherwise the children will also get anxious. Talk to children let them know what is happening in a language appropriate for their age e.g; younger children ..'Mom/Dad has a poorly head; sometimes when we have done too much it can affect the way we feel but with lots of kindness and rest he/ she should get better and we are all going to help...perhaps you can help too...we could make a get well card etc.'

(*) Mental Health assessment through GP always recommended. Depending on your authority they may be able to provide some support with the children but will always try to keep parent and child together otherwise it is too stressful for the children. There may be cases where it is not appropriate for children to be in the house. Always see what the MH team offer first and work your timetable around that. **I would not tell MH your plan as the more you offer the then more they back away and you want as much help as possible from this system because it may be minimal anyway.**

4. They are going to need basic food in the house so do **weekly/ fortnightly shopping**. Perhaps put one person in charge of a regular internet order. Check they have enough money to feed themselves and dependents. Ask for help from local charities or the community, if this is an issue, set up a 'fund me' page

5. Dialogue goes *"You don't need to worry about work, or shopping we have sorted this. You just need to focus on getting better and we are all here to help you do that."*

Nurture.

Their mind has collapsed, they are functioning at a child's level. So take a parenting role for now; are they washing themselves? Is their space relatively tidy? Are they are having enough water and hydrating themselves, are their clothes being washed?

You may have to share these activities (depending what local authority services have offered) between the help group you are organizing to start with. Once they are more stable start to get them to do some chores; introduce them slowly. If appropriate, **give them hugs and lots of kindness. Remember you are their advocate and parent between all of your group.**

Connection.

The help group you are creating should be people they know or trust as well qualified mental health professionals that may have been put on the case. Connection may also mean making sure their broadband/TV works or any communication device they may need to use when there are not people in the house.

Perhaps set up some positive you tube channels on the TV or get audio books if they cannot read. Leave the radio on. **Make sure it is a channel that is fun and not too much news which can be overwhelming.** Also make sure they have a phone line to a professional helpline and one of their friends every night. Just knowing that someone's phone is on is sometimes enough. Discuss what they are going to do if they do have time on their own. It is at this time that connection with other groups may be started e.g meditation groups/ gym/ football etc.

Structure.

A **rota** needs to be organized of visitors and it need to be around 2 to 4 hours of gentle activity weekly; whatever **they can cope with, not what you think they should be doing.** Remember: small, small steps. So reading to them; watching a film, small walks outside perhaps building up. They will need daily contact so try and involve them with people that they know and trust. **WRITE IT UP ON THE WALL/FRIDGE** so the person can clearly see who is coming in to the house and what activity e.g Nathan 4pm till 8pm on Mondays for film night.

Any appointments with a doctor or health professionals need to be attended. Any medication needs to be monitored. Ask the sufferer what they want; they don't have to take medication but if they think they need it monitor any sudden changes...leave a note so everyone knows what is going on. Introduce them to cooking / cleaning slowly, especially if they have children, it will be great for children to see some basic parenting coming back in.

When ready bring in therapy, either through the Doctors or privately, depending on what they can afford and how long they need to wait. **Their agitation may need to have calmed in order for therapy to be a viable option as concentration will be too poor. The nurturing and connection are more helpful at this stage before therapy will be beneficial otherwise the words and methods will not sink in and get processed.**

When they are feeling vaguely human, they may want to look up information on alternative treatments/nutrition. Helping them research this and perhaps writing notes for them will provide hope because now they are making plans and looking at other options; this is a great step.

If meds have been started then see how they are after 4 weeks. If in the first 4 weeks symptoms get worse consider changing the type of medication and communicate to the Doctor. Even though it can take up to 12 weeks significant side effects should not be suffered or tolerated it is making the already low feelings lower; this is simply too risky. **Ideally there should be someone in the house throughout the night, particularly if the person is suicidal.**

Recovery

All recovery has blips so try and use ***'remember'**..'*Remember the other day when you felt great..and we did this well that will happen again.

Recovery can be a bit up and down but it's an upward trajectory. Remind them of their journey: 'There are bound to be blips but you are improving all the time...remember'......

Ease off the care as they establish their independence again but make sure they know you are there on the phone. Keep them connected.

My most recent poem. Guess what? I finished the book and got anxiety. I had forgotten what it is like but I know I have been on this journey again through the words almost like a PTSD and that pesky little hippocampus is giving the Amygdala the wrong message. So of course I have to follow my own advice now. It is a journey and recovery can have its blips. Be strong my friends; **it will pass.**

When

When she takes you by surprise untimely
With heart pumped sleepless nights
When just the idea of her
Strikes your rib cage like a knife
the enemy you never had
Angry and bad
Never imagined such internal fights.

Such bravery you stand
Acting unhindered
Whilst within
She burns cinders
And outer shivery oversensitive skin
Voices so loud
Echoes shrill

Such physical churning
Whilst she cries and you could scream
Solar plexus, spleen
Overworked exhausted
Sweaty palms
She calms
and reveals
Frightened little one

Part of your soul
Brave warrior
Whole
Never alone

Let's put the hospitals and the community centres back in place but COMBINED; here's the plan, the vision, the reality that we can achieve.

Community Mental Health Centres; what every town/ community should have available that we can only dream of with our current government but let's imagine what it should be **because every thought creates a feeling that creates an action……**

Mental Health Community Centres with outdoor space/gym, music rooms/lessons and **beds** where **people can drop in without appointments**. Qualified staff man and support 24/7. Boundaries are agreed at the door by patients; **these boundaries are strict and are managed by everyone within the centre, including visitors**.

Doctors are available on call and if needed some patients (if deemed too severe) can get an **immediate assessment and may be allocated one of the many beds/ safe pods for the night.** Within the centres there are meditation sessions and other therapeutic methods available both individual or as a group.

Regular attendees who need support can also be volunteers (subject to appropriate checks) to help the staff manage the 'drop ins' and make suggestions on how to support them after all they have the most experience of how it feels.

Qualifications can be obtained to volunteers that the staff think have moved forward enough to potentially be a working member of staff. People who stay can chat to others that are well enough to go home if those people request a night call. Night call links are set up between attendees and staff to support each other throughout the night.

Some attendees will manage the garden where foraging and food is available. Attendees help build safety pods and relaxation huts in the garden with recycled materials and help of local builders who come in and teach attendees DIY skills.

Other skilled volunteers include gardeners, chefs, librarians and dancers…the list is endless. Let's keep adding to it.

Chapter 5

Please Breathe with The **'Upside Down'** Breathing Method

This is a short chapter to share a very basic technique with you that may help you calm down a little when you are agitated.

So far in this book I have told you my story in order to offer you hope.

Then we went into medication which is a VITAL to get right on this journey. If you don't want to take medication then explore the other possibilities discussed in Chapter 9. That is the first practical game changer. I presented a basic equation for you and your carers to follow **SNCS (Safety, Nurture, Connection, Structure)** in 4a.

In this chapter I want to tell you about one simple technique that can calm panic attacks. It was a simple method someone gave me whilst I was ill. The 'someone' happened to have experienced severe anxiety.

I knew she was telling me with true empathy. When she told me though I couldn't understand how it would work but it did and it's a simple method to take all the tension from around your heart and chest when you are agitated or having a panic attack. I've named it **the Upside Down breathing technique.**

Simply it will make you feel more in control of your body and has real physical and mental benefits.

Breathing is important. On recovery you may find that yogic breathing helps you along with the physical satisfaction of yoga. **Most people don't breathe properly.** This can cause anything from heart problems to extreme fatigue to anxiety. This is Deepak Chopra's explanation about yoga and In Chapter 8 you can discover more:

'The word yoga derives from the Sanskrit root yuj, which means union with the source of existence. Unity consciousness is also referred to as the state of enlightenment in which there is complete freedom from all conditioning and one is no longer constrained by habit, past experiences or "karma," and any forms of dogma or ideology. It is a state of spontaneous creativity, love, compassion, joy, and equanimity. These are also known as divine qualities.'

Yoga is about physically moving your body so your breath can travel through it in the best possible way. So, it's not so much about physical perfection but your body being in the right state to receive the Chi of life.

Breathing and breath is one of the most important parts of us. Lack of breath can lead to any disease because disease is 'dis' 'ease.' Your body is not at ease. Most people's bodies are not at ease but in anxiety this is tenfold. Mental health is harsh. Whilst your minds in turmoil you are experiencing panic attacks and heart palpitations.

I want you to follow this exercise which will help regulate the Oxygen around your body. It is fairly simple and I have sketched (roughly) the technique so, if it is easier, you can follow it visually.

So, let's put out the breathing method Start at this: get oxygen (O2) in your body stop focusing on the breath coming in through your mouth and trying to fill your chest. Yes, it does come in through your mouth but here's what you must do:

- Move to your focus to the solar plexus (see the diagram chakra 2) this is the soft bit right below where your ribs join in the middle of your chest.

- Now look at my diagrams and push 2 fingers gently into this spot.

- Breathe (or imagine) the breath is coming from below this point. It's easy, I promise you. When I say below this point; below the navel even from your pubic bone if you wish or base chakra.

- Despite you knowing breath comes in through your mouth or nose, with this pressure on your solar plexus you will feel the breath come from below your fingers all the way down from your base chakra.

- Again, just to stress the flow of breath comes from below your tummy button or even your genital area.

- The breath now will come up from below and it will push right up through your lower spine. You must imagine the breath is heading up into your upper back rather than your front.

- Keep your fingers pushed into the solar plexus, and as the spine opens and pushes back it will then push forward onto your chest pushing it out easily.

- This breath starts from below the navel. It takes the breath from the worrying head, tight chest and heart and focuses it elsewhere and it gives you a break and hopefully helping you relax.

- This is your break. If it doesn't work you haven't failed by the way. I'm sure it will work to calm you but the most important thing is push your fingers into the solar plexus if you're not getting the full breath.

- This pressure point feels like a valve opening and allowing O2 into your body. Sometimes I just tap this area lightly and the imaginary valve opens letting the oxygen through to complete the full breath.

- We often feel we are not getting enough breathe and then go into panic mode this will turn that feeling on its head literally.
- Once the breath has stretched you back and starts pushing out your chest cavity you can imagine the Oxygen going up the back of the neck and flowing round the head at same time as it pushes the chest up. This feels great. It allows some freshness into that over worked and exhausted brain, yes some of this is imagination but by opening the body to allow oxygen in that oxygen will get into the blood stream and hit those important areas quickly.

More points to add;

- What you also need to know is that when you are having a panic attack and your chest is tight as well as this method remember that your body will always make sure you breathe. If there is not enough oxygen to the brain you will pass out and your body will continue to breathe on its own. That knowledge in itself gave me some peace.

- Once you have mastered this method and still using it to amplify the deep breathing you can bring in the 'BOX' breathing method which is simply 1. Breathe in for 4 seconds. 2. Hold for 4 seconds. 3.Breathe out for four seconds then 4. Hold for 4 seconds start again.

- I don't use the above method as it makes me focus too much but it really works for some people. What I find really useful about the 'upside down' breath is once I've done it a few times it seems to just flow naturally without me thinking about it.

- Also, if comfortable, start to hear the flow of this breath by sounding your breath so you can hear it travel through your body. Many people do this in yoga classes to control and maximize their breathe. It can also be relaxing. It can be described as a 'Hu' sound see How to Breathe in Yoga Poses: 5 Transformative Pranayama ...www.yogajournal.com/practice/importance-breath-yoga#:~:text=TRY%20IT%E2%80%A6.

- When you get into a position where you are relaxed and breathing well to take this a step further look into the Wim Hof method which makes you understand the connection between the primal brain, the mind and breathing https://www.wimhofmethod.com/ His methods look at putting the bodies through extreme temperatures; this does not mean you have to sit in ice although Hof believes that anyone normal person can learn to adapt their bodies to extremities. His breathing methods are extremely valuable for controlling our mind and anxiety, I would say don't practice his faster

meditations until you are ready. The method can feel uncomfortable to start with but if you get through it you will realise it calms your physiological system of anxiety quickly and as a daily habit can reduce inflammation and prevent disease. ***Right in the middle of an anxiety episode the ability to use Wim Hof's methods have been a life saver for me.*** You will love his gentle energy. He is quite a *dude* (Wim Hof) and he really has been 'through the mill' too.
https://www.bing.com/videos/search?q=wim+hoff+breathing+technique&docid=607993508930600203&mid=24FE87735A8E

- Of course' a regular activity to get involved with to help with anxiety and depression is **cold water swimming** which increases the endorphins and anti -inflammatory reactions in the body once you have submerged yourself. You may have to build up to longer levels of actually cold water dipping or shower blasts. In Cornwall there are many groups who are doing cold water swimming and reporting amazing effects. As a community activity to connect with others this may also be helpful. Read about it and connect with local groups on the following link;
https://outdoorswimmer.com/blogs/swim-positive

- I recently broke my leg quite badly whilst surfing in too shallow water. Once I had made a call to my dear friend who came and collected my son and I knew the process and the fact that I don't have to re-mortgage my house in this country for an operation, I was able to take the incident within my stride. I'm sure it wasn't as easy for the Coastguards who had to carry me up a steep slope off the beach. In the hospital my blood pressure was low and the nurse kept having to test my pulse and breathing as she said it was taking me a long time to take a breath. My Oxygen levels within my body were excellent. She said I must do a lot of exercise (I don't, just a moderate amount). I was simply breathing properly and making sure that that breath was entering every part of my upper and lower chest cavity so that my body in turn receives the correct amount of Oxygen. The breathing also kept me calm.

- If you can master a strong breathing technique this is a way of calming your body sending signals to the brain that all is ok. It also benefits the immune system and heart as well as reduce inflammation.

- As I said before, the upside down method works for me because once I have done it a few times I feel it just flows naturally; focussing too much on breathing (like the Box method) has made me too conscious of my breath but now that I have mastered Wim Hof , I am a total fan. Good luck and keep breathing!

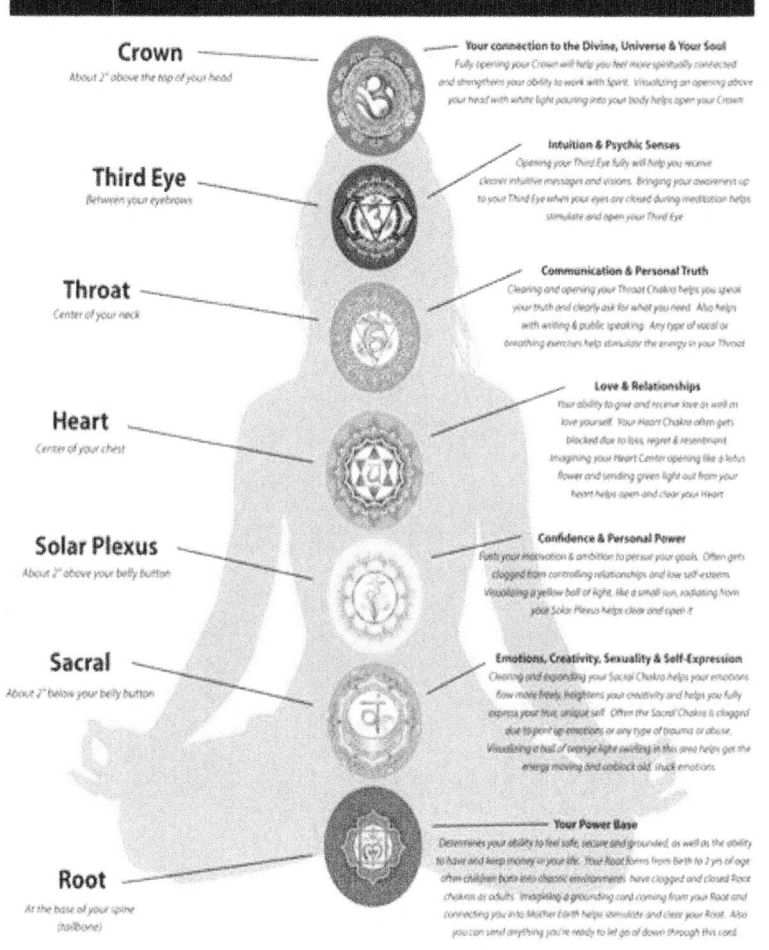

Illustration 1 the Solar Plexus is the yellow wheel at the centre where the release valve is to allow oxygen to flow in the body by 'upside down' breathing.

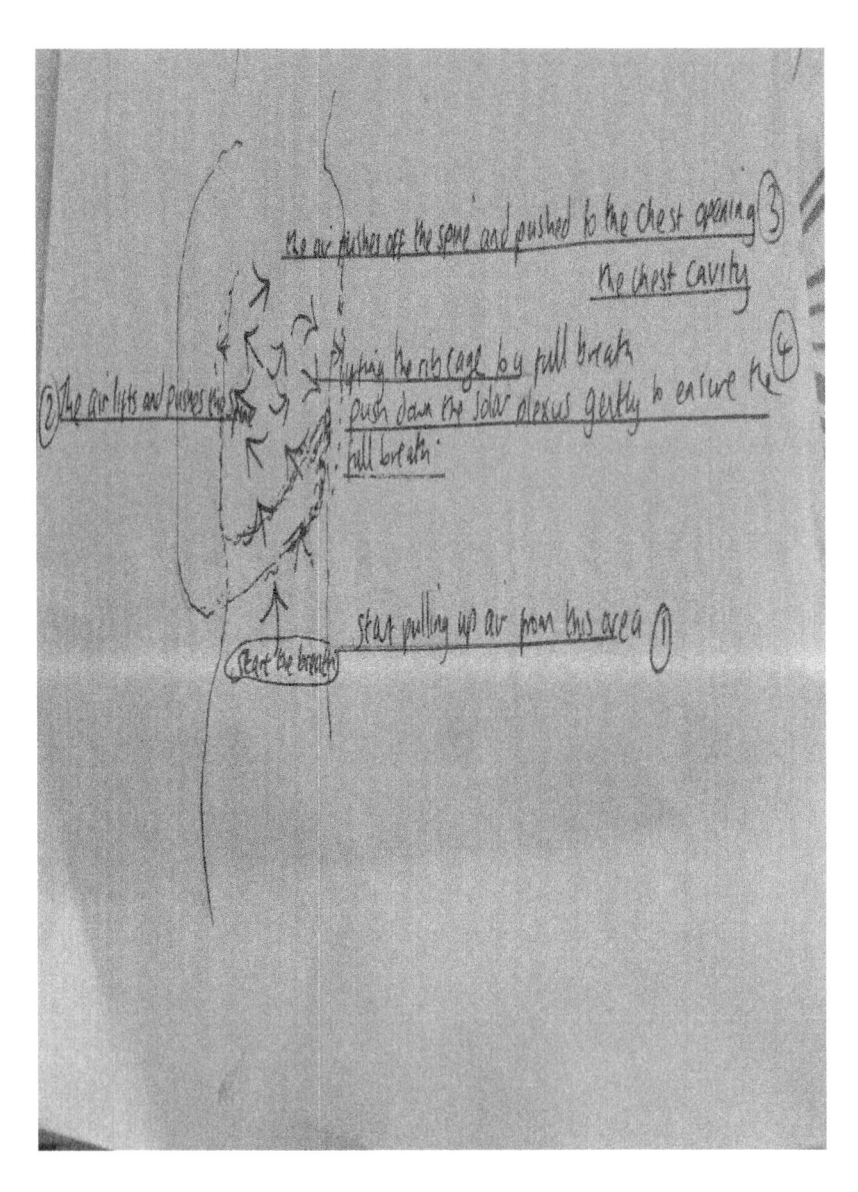

Illustration 2 a brief sketch of the process involved in Upside Down breathing.

Sorry For My Breakdown

This is my life

From such carefree.

But the free turned into a care

that got OCD

then anxiety

I'm not a Syrian refugee

Hopeless,

Dying in the snow

And for all that

I know.

And yet this bully

This despair

Still consumes

Everywhere.

So I don't care.

Just manage each minute

Of Fear!

A bubble an observatory

A helpless hopeless zone

That people have started to avoid

So now it's time

To be alone.

'Snap out of it Stupid

I slap myself in the face

Mindfulness, Avoidance, distraction

Trying every trick in the book.

Whispers around that I just

Want a reaction.

That I am just keeping myself in this torture chamber

And whatever your good advice

Your frustration with me

I have already told

Myself that twice

(In the last second).

Constant wear on my health

A fool destroying herself!

Chapter 6

<u>Unlock your Life Jigsaw</u>

We all have a' Yarn,' we all have a story; this is what the aboriginals used to call 'Yarning' -sitting round the fire' telling your story, creating connection, weaving a tapestry of people's lives enabling the elders and tribe members to support you with who you were.

Our world has become fragmented for many reasons and stopped this beautiful tapestry becoming interwoven with others; **understanding we are all connected to the same source is an integral part of preventing mental health decline.**

But now I am going to take you on your own journey through mine.

Welcome to your jigsaw; this could fundamentally change the way you operate and view your life. If you're in a tough situation this may just be the key to putting your demise into an understanding that will make you start the changes needed.

The reason this chapter is called 'the jigsaw' is because we all have the ability to understand how we were put together; this means we all have the ability to break and rearrange our own jigsaws as we choose.

I am going to tell you about my jigsaw; the experiences I had that created the views, feelings and emotions and which effected how I reacted to the outside world. If you follow this puzzle then you can re trace your own emotional patterns.

I'm showing you how to unravel the tapestry of experiences until you come to your own 'hurts' 'the lack ofs', the abuse, the neglect, and of course you will learn the truths of your greater moments and experiences.

You are reading this because you are a modern emotional Viking Warrior of your own thought system, because you want to question them, to change and improve your own paths and ultimately fight for you.

We are all intricate tapestries of emotional successes and emotional 'fuck ups' that deeply embed within our beings and take front line as a tool in our egoic mind. **In our everyday life they show up in our actions and sometimes self-sabotaging patterns.**

These patterns create empty Vacuums that we spend our whole lives trying to fill relentlessly and unsuccessfully.

Our vacuums are the hurts that we constantly try to fill the identity we associate ourselves with in order to be 'whole.' The vacuums can never be filled so they suck all our efforts away make us repeat these patterns till they exhaust us.

These little internal demons have us running in circles, choosing the wrong partners, not valuing ourselves and sometimes becoming ill.

By seeing and understanding them we can honour them without pouring all our energy into them and STOP the continuing struggle.

We know they are there; they are part of our makeup **but they are not us.** We don't have to let them destroy us. There are always going to be times when you may slip back into trying to fill their voids, but before you know it you will learn to recognise them. This is what this chapter is for; to recognise them and know that they hang around with you **but they are not you!**

Let me tell you about my life and show you the vacuums I developed. The emotional defaults that would lead me into negative pointless journeys. You may recognise your own patterns, or you may need to write down your journey so you can recognise them.

My suggestion is that **if anything crops up in your head about your childhood; stop and write it down**; don't get involved in it; just observe it. Then go back to reading this chapter.

These memories may make you feel happy or sad but let those feelings pass and once on paper, there it is your recognition significant to your emotional journey and **ultimately the unique jigsaw you created of you.**

No matter how traumatic, or even joyous these memories, just observe them observe and allow your feelings about them and then keep reading. Remember I say this throughout the book.

You are not your trauma. You are not any less of a person if someone abused you but learning to untwine the feelings that you have allowed to become you has defined the way you function. It is now time to release and nurture all of this; The path to self-love my friend.

So here is my life unravelled; I'm going to surprise you by saying it was not a hard life. I had a privileged upbringing and that is part of the problem created. I never realised I had issues because I had a roof over my head, food and money. How could there be problems?

My name is Morag and when I was 43 I had a nervous breakdown. After surviving it, **I didn't realise that before the breakdown I had very little regard for myself.** The regard I showed was a false confidence; a reliance on the outer opinions of me to form me.

I was born in winter 1972. I was a mistake; my (*) Mom always used to joke about this with affection; the result of using 'The Cap' contraceptive shield I managed to sneak my way in this world. My Mother would always say, despite being a mistake, I was her favourite and today through tragedy and joy we remain close. I was surely loved.

(*) 'Mom' is how I address my Mother and is used throughout it is the colloquial form from the Midlands where I was brought up, like 'Mam' or 'Mum'

My parents, Joyce and John, already had two children: a boy Tim aged 5 and Clare aged 3. When I came into the world my Mom was training to be a teacher; my Dad was starting his own engineering business. Both were career hard working individuals that got on the right side of the then Labour government, followed by the Thatcher government. They had both started to successfully carve their way into the world.

It was probably a bit of a shock to have me, considering both my parents, intelligent working class people, were pushing forward with their careers after already having two children.

Even then though, I think cracks were showing. I recently learned at a reunion of my Dad's family that my parents had a 'dry' wedding; in other words, a wedding with no alcohol!

My Dad came from a farming family on the borders of Shropshire; he was one of five; the fourth born. His Mother went into hospital when he was 5 for a routine procedure after being unwell for a while; she never returned.

There may have been one bad screw up, but no one will know because in those days there wasn't as much accountability as there is today. His Father (my Grandpa,) never got over the death of his wife, he couldn't cope with the sudden loss and responsibilities this tragedy had brought and as a result my Dad was brought up by his siblings and was close to his only brother Fred.

All of them grew up fairly stable, except for my Dad, who started to binge drink at an early age. My Uncle Fred recalled coming back from the army and being refused a drink because they had mistaken him for his mischievous younger brother at the bar.

The hurt of his Mother's loss was in his family, unexpressed and he learned to express it (badly of course) through addiction; his drug of choice was alcohol. None of his siblings had this problem.

My Mom was brought up in poverty the eldest of four; her Mom (my Gran) handmade all their clothes and worked tirelessly for her children. My Mom and her sister June both trained as teachers. My youngest Aunt became a secretary for my Dad's business. She herself became addicted to alcohol and cigarettes and died in her 50s.

We moved house in rented accommodation a few times, until in the late 70s my Dad bought a building plot and employed some of the builders he knew, and a big red brick five bedroom house was built in the 'posher' part of town, close to acres of woodland known as Cannock Chase.

My early memories of childhood were quite straightforward. Meals were round the table and me, my brother and sister had fun and civilized conversation. I was often the object of my brother and sister's ridicule; they used to call me 'Mrs Ubble' for some reason because the selection of clothes I chose out of the fancy dress box reminded them of an old lady so they created a Mrs U; yes we had a fancy dress box, it was wonderful.

Before the red brick-house I remember me my brother and sister, all being embedded in the lounge of our rented accommodation at Uncle Tom Pillsbury's. We all had Chicken Pox. Later we would blame our chicken pox scars on Mom's choice of itchy blankets!

Uncle Tom Pillsbury's was our transitional flat, before the red brick building of our middle -class destination. It was in effect a maisonette. We lived above Tom Pillsbury and his wife and they looked after Tom's ailing Mother. Our energy, as a young family must have invigorated their house and they always seemed very kind and fond of us all.

I remember their beautiful garden, even though in the suburbs of a developing ex mining town, was a little haven surrounded by green shrubs and trees. You wouldn't know there was a dairy opposite and a big car park and depot ready for the milkmen, who used to trail around in their slow gently buzzing electric vehicles delivering milk in glass bottles; all acceptable, all recyclable. A few years later these systems were made extinct in favour of convenience which has come to put our world out of balance.

In this little haven at Uncle Tom Pillsbury's my Father used to be working a lot then. I had accepted that this was important, my Mother still struggling between her teaching career and bringing up three children. Both were hard working. Having my Dad about felt beautiful, he was the icing on the cake. Even though he was loveable I sometimes felt his presence was a gift to treasure only available at certain times somehow inconspicuous. My Mother's energy was abundant and available always in those early years.

Sometimes at night at Uncle Tom's my imagination would take hold of me. I shared a bedroom with my brother and sister; a bunk and a single bed , and whilst they were asleep, feeling scared, I would make the treacherous journey up another floor to my parents' bed and they would make a space for me in the middle of their bed. How beautiful this haven was; I felt safe.

I also remember, despite this great satisfaction with my childhood, I had a fear that came out of nowhere. Protected in Uncle Tom Pillsbury's garden, on sunny days I used to watch the clouds. If they became too close or too vigorous at the age of 5 or 6, I developed the notion that these clouds were going to fall out the sky and destroy us all. I couldn't tell anyone of this fear (I don't know why).

One day the skies bulged with clouds despite the bright sun, my Mom was happy snoozing and sunbathing in the garden. Despite my Mom's relaxed persona the clouds to me were a threat I ran inside shutting the door behind me. I then realised in a panic that I needed to tell the ones I loved what was happening. The door seemed to lock and I couldn't get out. I felt terror like I have never felt. I remember screaming. I was trapped without my family whilst the impending doom of nature reigned down and I was helpless to change it.

I am sure I wasn't there for that long but Uncle Tom Pillsbury and my Mom came to my rescue, reassuring me all would be ok. I never shared these intense fears and emotions. I am not sure at the time within families this was encouraged either. This was a habit which continued as I got older; keeping worries 'under wrap.'

When we did finally move to the red brick house this was the time of growing up becoming more independent. This was our home we now lived in a pretty much mortgage free, five bedroomed house thanks to My Mom and Dad. We lived in abundance; we could eat what we wanted.

We used to go and explore the woods when my cousins visited; my Mom's closer sister June with her son Niall and Laura. We would almost be totally independent: me at 8 or 9, my sister 3 years older, off to the Chase building dens, pulling up sledges when the guaranteed snows fell in December. There were no real time constraints just back before dark; no mobiles or messages just a faith that all would be ok. These were all beautiful days.

You can see this was all pretty good for me but as the youngest, I think from the age of seven and moving into the red brick house (that I still love and hate), one thing always started to become less and less; My Father's presence. It became less and less until I noticed at twelve or thirteen years of age, when my hormones were kicking in, that my Father felt like an inconvenience in my life.

The sound of the key aiming but often missing the lock to our front door during evening times, was actually incredibly anxiety inducing, chaotic and disturbing for me. Stumbling in through the door, was not the beautiful man who I knew as my Father but a drunken swearing mess. Never sexually or physically harmful to us, but a different character shouting out abuse and swearing, sometimes falling down or burning food he tried to cook. I could never sleep till he got into bed in case he set the house on fire. It was all a lot to try and deal with when you had School the next day.

My house was pretty open and sociable; my Mom, by this time, was tired she had partially given up and was just about coping. A career, three teenagers and a drunken husband. She was doing a grand job to still cook us nutritious meals but emotionally I think she had nothing left to give. I don't think you realise the monstrous task this is until you become a parent yourself.

The cupboards were always full of food; my Dad was still managing to run a business before he hit the pub; so we sort of became posh delinquents, inviting friends round eating what we wanted to. It was all there. Our house was free for visitors as long as it wasn't at night.

I started venturing out to the pubs at 14; alcohol became my thing, not every day but at weekends other teenagers would gladly join me in over indulging and escaping in alcohol, anaesthetising their souls from the chaos at home.

I never had one adult talk to me about the path I was taking. My Mom was just knee deep in shit and just floating her family to even realise problems were emerging. I now realise that years of a drunken husband, three children and a teaching career was overloading her into her own depression.

The love was there but the self- care was not. No one understood emotional vulnerability because by the time the 80s had hit, value in society had been placed on the exciting wealth growth that some were experiencing; the acceleration of the wealth my parents must have gained must have made them feel they should be grateful for their lot.

Emotions were put on the back burner and questioning emotions would have been thought of as almost ungrateful because of the abundance we appeared to have.

Duran Duran on a yacht portraying the high life, Madonna pushing out female power and talking about virginity openly, electronic keyboards hitting the emotional beats of that progressive era.

This was probably where I was learning to understand my emotions. I was drawn more towards Nick Kershaw's sombre tones than Wham's good life vibes. I was an attractive blonde with pointed leather pale mint brogue type shoes or pixie boots and an over sprayed mullet.

If there is one tune that sums up that era for me it was 'Everybody Wants to Rule The World' by Tears For Fears. Too many of us in fact wanted to rule the world; the rise of materialism and possession had become our god. Whilst some people were experiencing property surges on a roller coaster ride of wealth, others were fighting for the survival of their families. Still today the gaps rise further and only a few got to rule the world whilst the rest of us started to realise this high life had taken its toll on Mother Earth.

Before rocketing into teenagehood, I remember one night when I was about 10. It was a significant moment in my life. I was at my friends Maxine's a short walk away but I needed to go home. I rang home and my Mom proudly announced my Dad would walk up and come and collect me; for some reason my Dad was at home and sober.

I started to walk down and I saw my Dad, his big frame in his big grey quilted coat; he loved me so much I know that. He put his arm around me and we had a chat about this and that.

I did not tell him that this was a rare moment for me. I had no understanding either of the destructive effects of addiction and emotional trauma that could spill out through generations. **What I** *knew was in that moment that my beautiful Father was doing what I wished he would always have done; protecting me under the clear starry sky. This had to be a warmth and feeling I would seek like a drug (sometimes wrongly) for a lot of my life.*

I also remember from that moment of normality to most moments of chaos. Once, my dad had found out I had got a boyfriend; I was young perhaps 13, and the boy was 15. It wasn't serious, yet my dad sat there totally pissed and whatever prison of suffering he was coming from his way of communicating his concern was "Have you started your periods yet?"

I had, but had failed to tell either of my parents. I felt a shame at growing up and I guess things were just too hectic to sit and have a conversation about womanhood.

I answered my Dad's question "No" I lied

"Well, that's good" he slurred "at least you can't get pregnant!"

I wasn't sexually active then but somehow that comment made me feel cheap and uncherished, and I think it had a profound effect on the way I felt about myself.

I was quite shocked that he would talk about me in this way but then I realised this is the distortion excess alcohol can induce. However rather than being repulsed by his addiction I was already starting to imitate his behaviour by binge drinking in an attempt to soothe my wounds.

I love this description of addiction by Pema Chodron;

"All addictions come when we meet our edge; we feel we have to soften it, pat it with something and we become addicted to whatever it is that seems to soften the pain."

I want to tell you that during my recovery a lovely man called Mick made me realise that children of alcoholics become highly sensitive adults. This has been well documented and attributed to their life experience, **always desperately running round trying to make everything normal in a chaotic world. They want to make everything ok. This results in not being able to hold boundaries easily.** Can you recognise this in yourself; boundaries are an important skill to have. I am still learning even now but because I know my boundaries are poor, I can pick them up before I make myself too vulnerable to others.

This also made me a prime vulnerable ticking time bomb for controlling men.

Alcoholic parents are not available for their children when they drink; and children of alcoholics become over sensitive and anxious to potentially chaotic situations which of course creates anxious responses.

Mick also made me realise why all my life I had been drawn to beautiful but melancholic music such as the haunting tones of Nick Drake and Leonard Cohen in my 20s.

More interestingly, why I feel sick when I see black and white movies. They were usually on the TV on a Sunday when my Dad would be sober at home to try and act like we were a 'normal family.' There was always a melancholic atmosphere in the air and a black and white movie on TV or (even worse) *Worzel Gummidge* and Aunt Sally; *Worzel Gummidge* screwing different heads on and Aunt Sally stiffly walking round like a corpse. If you can remember that programme, you will understand, it was surreal to say the least.

Well, there was my Dad with his rare sober head on but for some reason it was melancholy to know this was the calm before the whisky storm starting again the next day. Anxiety would heighten when he literally rolled into the house in a calamity of drunkenness.

At this point I want to say DO NOT and I mean DO NOT get too sad about this story. *This is not a victim story I am not a victim.*

Everyone was a victim, including my Father, if we go back to Pema's definition of addiction; **addiction is a futile attempt to fill the bottomless vacuums of the pain we have.**

When I started to recover from my darkest moments my jigsaw and the vacuums it contained made sense. My past was exactly what it was, it was certainly not as bad as some people's childhoods but it doesn't matter *how* painful it is; *our past is only a problem when we continue to allow it to cause us pain.*

In the next chapter I give you some pointers when you know your own vacuums and in Chapter 8 some very special teachers that can further develop your understanding of your own journeys. I whole heartedly recommend them and they are all in the reference and recommendations at the back.

I haven't spoken about this another teacher Byron Katy though as I wanted to focus on Eckart Tolle amongst others and this lady comes next as her work is about letting go. She is worth looking up and one of her great lessons is;

"If you try to argue with your past you will lose 100% of the time."

I find that statement phenomenal; it took me a while to sink in to what those words really mean. *Releasing yourself from your past whilst still being able to be an observer and honour that part of your journey can ultimately release you from a great deal of pain.* It may be your freedom. I will touch on it more in the next chapter.

I do remember ironically funny moments with my Dad. Trying to get him into his pyjamas and in bed whilst he fell over on the floor several times. He would be laughing and giggling, sometimes swearing. I would laugh along but underneath my heart was churning waiting for a tragedy.

The lack of this nurture found me seeking nonexistence solace in sources like alcohol, risky behaviours and insecure relationships throughout my life.

So, this is where the gaps started to appear, on the surface a middle- class family with everything they need. Underneath anxiety past 7.30pm a shy sensible intelligent man turns into Frankenstein, and no one wants to draw attention to this.

No one questioned the dysfunctionality and the chaos that was occurring. There was not any support or questioning then, we were attempting to sweep a hippopotamus under the carpet.

I remember my Dad; his big grey coat he smelt of smoke; I loved smelling his smoky coat.

The day he died my beautiful Mom was away. She came back after receiving the news and picked up the grey quilted XL grey anorak he had slung on the bottom of the stairs. Through her tears she pushed her face into this last living vibration of him, she smelt and felt the essence of my Father.

He had been absent from her for so long and now the absence was eternal. I stood at the top of the stairs feeling totally responsible for his death. *A theme that would repeat throughout my life; a theme that would show itself in continual apologies and feeling guilty about the most trivial things. Essentially apologising for me.*

From an early age I became drawn towards young men that I guess were bad. I would say I had a preference that I was a good girl from a middleclass family unlike some of the 'slags' that had given themselves away to men. The reality was is that I could be classed as a slag too; not that definition has any relevance or meaning in defining women but in my childhood it was rife.

At age fourteen to fifteen I was dibbling and dabbling with boys sexually. I had no idea I was attractive as I was; now I know I am both inside and out. Looks should not be an important measure of a person but teenagers are obsessed with this aspect of themselves. Feeling attractive on the inside and out in a healthy way is a hard balance for parents to get right with their children.

This is no criticism but to **tell your children they are worth something is paramount**. I just don't think my parents were ever brought up to instil this into people so **I learned to gather myself and who I was about from the opinions of others**. There was a lot of pressure to conform and look how I thought others expected of me.

I can honestly say now that having a breakdown reversed this process and I have learned to love myself from within, so others people's opinions aren't paramount. What a shame it took a breakdown to realise this.

Despite being under the illusion I was pure, by fourteen onwards I had got into binge drinking; this led to male attention and getting into the wrong relationships. *Smoking and drinking at weekends were my cushions to fill the void of insecurity, but as we know they never do.*

It was a 'mish mash' of me being a party girl but actually wanting to please men and make them happy. Some people have told me I was stunning; life is not about how you look but my inner essence was not nurturing or admiring, like many young women, **it was highly critical of me.**

I needed to look in the mirror to make sure I looked as I needed to, add makeup, add new clothes. There was no peace of mind or acceptance that I had so much, when simply I felt so little for myself. I feel the pressure for young women now is even greater as I have mentioned in Chapter 4 **"With more pressure from social media young women are hormone injected, fully waxed ready to serve young men's high demands: not (in my opinion) the basis for a healthy society."**

At fifteen I started a relationship with Matty, a Greek Cypriot, because of family tradition he would have to marry a Greek girl. I **was already going for partners who weren't fully available to me like my Father, who was not available either.**

I didn't fall in love with Matty, even though he was lovely, my choices weren't about me they were just about solace from the lack of male nurture I was missing in my life. Matty was pretty keen but my ability to love anyone was limited.

I was with Matty on the night my father passed away, immediately I want to say it was my fault. That is my default feeling my mind had tortured me with for many years. It still does but I have learned to listen, forgive nurture and release it.

My Father had become a dysfunctional stranger in my life; as much as I loved him, he was someone I avoided now. His pain dispersed through continual alcohol abuse. I wish in the 80s we had been more clear and defined about the help we can offer these people. Maybe my Dad was suffering the intense anxiety I had felt when I finally broke? If he was anxious, alcohol may have seemed the only solution for him, sadly we will never know.

I was free to do exactly what I wanted; this was the problem. My Mom cared and begged me to stop going out so much. As a Mom now I can feel her pain, but the control had been lost through the dysfunctionality that was an everyday part of our family life.

In May 1987 my Mother was away and my Dad turned up sober; I had planned a night of getting trashed with my friends. I was a tall slim fifteen year old blonde wearing baggy cotton trousers a tight top and medium high black heels. I must have looked very grown up. I wondered if Dad felt a sad distance between him and his daughter with so many misunderstandings. **I wonder now if he realised I was seeking his nurture and approval through empty vacuums of young men's attention to prove my own worthiness?**

Whilst my Dad saw me as beautiful, I didn't. As I mentioned I was obsessed with looking in the mirror, maybe more so than most teenager girls. Some view this as vain for me it was a validation that I looked OK for the outer world and only my reflection could determine this. Inside I have come to realise now I was a fragile entity.

My poor Dad had a headache he seemed very unwell; the giveaway was **he was sober** and it was before 7pm. He must have been frightened and I asked him if I should call the Doctor. He refused and said perhaps wait till the morning and see how he was then.

Part of me must have felt 'fuck you' why should I care for you, but I watched him sat in the kitchen struggling to inhale a cigarette and pretend everything was normal. He was my Dad; I knew he was in pain.

I knew he was scared and selfishly I went and continued my debauchery of indulging and wanting the need for male attention that was sadly about to end.

During that evening whilst I was drunk I cried badly; no one understood but when they asked what was wrong I told them that for certain 'I thought my Dad was dying.'

He did die, Matty did not get his way and I stumbled home drunk that night. It was a usual event I was somehow trying to escape and get wrecked.

When I got home, I heard my Father in bed, he was breathing quite fast; I wasn't comfortable with this but too drunk to worry I stole a few notes from his back pockets. I often did this it was payback; punishment for him not being there for me. Cash tucked away in his tobacco smelling trousers he hung up on the rocking chair, the same rocking chair that seemed to rock on its own when I found his hard blue body the next day. Rigor mortis had set in. I screamed so loud and as I tried to turn his stiff body over I burst a blood vessel in my cheek.

My sister was also home and she came in after. My brother at university, after hearing the news went missing for a few hours and continued the next few years with insomnia and depression.

My Mom returned to the house distraught. Suddenly the drunken stranger in our house had become a hero to be remembered. Our lives would never be the same again.

I remember listening to the sober haunting music of Joan Armatrading 'Love and Affection,'

"I am not alone but I'm open to affection, East or West where's the best for romancing across the floor cheek to cheek..."

Here was the start of my journey to ease my pain with the search of a replacement male figure in my life; *little did I know that I had no emotional tools or foundations to understand what a healthy relationship looked like, I only knew that I had grown up with my Father in pain and absent emotionally from my life.*

We had become a middle -class family but I would have happily exchanged money for some of my Father's sober time and nurture.

My Father John Percy Morgan 1941 to 1987; A man with so much potential but lost to pain and addiction.

My main emotional vacuum was Male nurture!

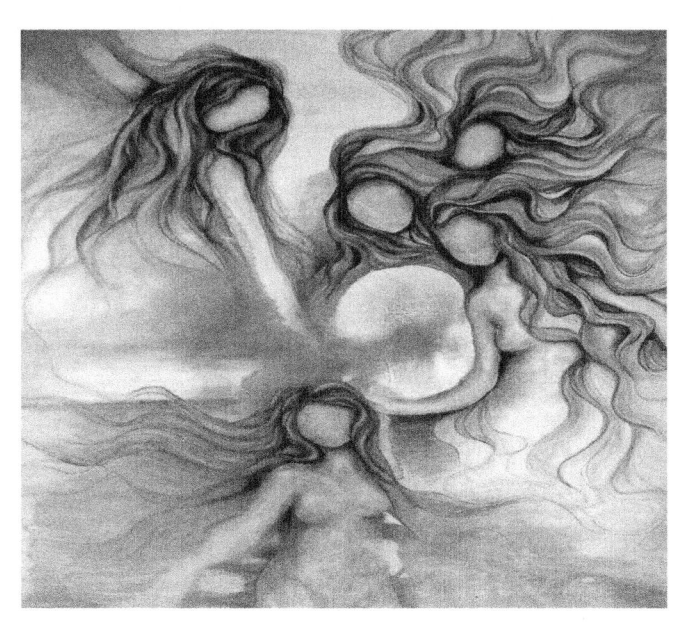

Wild Woman Sisterhood
NotoStpvlotnemcsmibeart o4e,c 20mn19rufgeadr ·

I think it was Brene Brown who told a story about a village where all the women washed clothes together down by the river. When they all got washing machines, there was a sudden outbreak of depression and no one could figure out why.

It wasn't the washing machines in and of themselves. It was the absence of time spent doing things together. It was the absence of community.

Friends, we've gotten so independent.

We're "fine" we tell ourselves even when in reality we're depressed, we're overwhelmed, we're lonely, and we're hurting. "We're fine, we're just too busy right now" we say when days, weeks, months, and years go by without connecting with friends. I'm fine, I'm fine, I'm fine. It's so easy to say even when it's not true.

We've become so isolated and it's hard to know how to get back. It's so hard to know how to even begin to build the kind of relationships our hearts need. And I think in our current culture, it's just not as organic as it once was. It's more work now.

Because you know, we have our own washing machines. We don't depend on each other to do laundry, or cook dinner, or raise babies anymore. We don't really depend on each other for much of anything if we're being honest.

In Brene Brown's book Braving the Wilderness, she says that being lonely effects the length of our life expectancy similar to smoking 15 cigarettes a day. I don't say that to freak anyone out, but to let you know that the longing for connection is LEGIT. I think we've treated friendship like a luxury for far too long; friendship isn't a luxury, it's a necessity.

We don't want it. We kind of need it.

Be independent. Be proud of it. But be an independent woman who realizes the value and the importance of opening the door to other good women. You can do it alone, but you don't have to. Islands are only fun for so long. There is true magic when women come together and hold hands and share ideas and share stories and struggles and endless bowls of salsa. You use your gifts, and I'll use mine, and then we'll invite that girl over there who brings a completely different set of skills to the table we are building, and we'll watch together as something miraculous unfold.

Author: Amy Weatherly, Art Darcy Lee.

Happy Ever After

When the world is bright

No agitation/ internal prison

Head so tight

When there is no fight

For I have lost my soul and laughter

And yet shaking

I read my boy

'Happy Ever after!

And he knows;

their beautiful energy

Knows when happiness disguises misery.

Never has life seemed such a gift

From this deep dark hole

Never has a conversation I hear

(about the weather)

Feel so enlightened and

Such a far to reach goal.

left; 2016 the start of recovery.

Chapter 7

<u>The Vacuums and the path out of the shame cycle.</u>

The vacuums we have are an important part of the patterns we unconsciously choose. Thoughts are very powerful and in the next chapter we discuss the thought process and bring in spiritual teachers who can guide you into good mind practices.

The vacuums of our lives produce a lot of raw and negative emotions which often manifest themselves in **lack of self-worth**.

At the end of this chapter, as well as discussing and recognising your vacuums, I have given an example of the method to lead you out of these self-destructive ways and more importantly show you how significantly different I am after my breakdown.

Read the 'shame cycle' and apply it to yourself. It will stop anyone from being able to deplete or undermine any positivity in your life because you will not lay all your vulnerability on a plate for them to destroy. Firstly, let's just recap on what a vacuum is…

A quick reminder from the last chapter 'our vacuums are emotional self-sabotaging patterns that we spend our whole lives trying to fill relentlessly and unsuccessfully.'

Our vacuums are the hurts that we constantly try to fill, but the vacuums can never be filled, so they suck all our efforts away making us repeat patterns until they exhaust us. They prevent us from ourselves and lead to physical and mental exhaustion and sometimes illness.

By seeing and understanding them we can honour them without pouring all our energy into them and **STOP** the continuing negative patterns.

Whilst I cover the most common vacuums, or the ones related to my experience, you may recognise other vacuums that are unique for you. In general, there are a small amount that will capture so many emotional experiences of our childhoods and provide us with some of the keys to the emotional journeys we have taken.

The main Vacuum I carried all my life was 'Father Nurture' the need or craving for male attention and protection. I also carried with me a food vacuum associated with weight gain or loss as well as a health vacuum, commonly associated with 'Health Anxiety'.

Some traits, habits and patterns I still carry out but the difference is I understand, accept, nurture, observe and keep them within a healthy parameter. Ignoring or not understanding them and letting them fester can encourage growth till Boom! One day they are out of control.

See if you can relate to any of these in reflection of your own journey:

Male Nuture Vacuum.

The biggest vacuum of all for many and the reasons I had made so many bad relationship decisions. The guys that wanted to save me and would tell me the stories were usually manipulative and controlling; scratch under the surface and you will see **their narcissistic habits that ironically are just survival patterns to preserve their misunderstood journeys.** This reminds me of the words of James Baldwin.

"I Imagine one of the reasons people cling to their hates so stubbornly is because they sense, once hate is gone, they will be forced to deal with pain.'

('Me and My House, Harpers NOV 55).

Hate and anger are just a cover for fear and the same can be said for some of our own habitual patterns we develop from our childhood experiences to envelope the truth away. *When a storm hits, the envelope becomes saturated and weak, disintegrating to reveal its contents.*

If you learn and recognise these patterns and the circumstances that created them; you will observe why you are choosing to be drawn into this energy.

With my Father absent in my life from a very young age I was desperately seeking to be saved from my pain. I was also grossly inadequate to provide all the healthy emotions needed within a relationship. However, through the teachings of spiritual masters such as Deepak Chopra we can learn that **the only true love is 'self-love'** and from there other love can blossom.

We have to nurture the seeds within ourselves instead of trying to ask another to grow the blossom; they never will. They can tell you that you are the blossom, but this can change at any time and **we can never have emotional stability if it relies on another's opinion of us.**

This vacuum also coincides with my vulnerability from a chaotic house and having one parent who was an alcoholic, my boundaries were weak; an undeserved gift given to us by our alcoholic or addicted parent or parents.

Whatever the abuse; mental, physical or emotional, **children of alcoholics are exposed to unstable emotions and unpredictable environments.** When that drinking glass comes out or, in my case, the parent walks in drunk, anything can happen. The child of an alcoholic finds their own emotions and needs are lost and internalized. They become the peace keepers the 'make everything ok' as their feelings are lost, so too are their boundaries.

Children of alcoholics ask,' why is my family not normal'? From that, guilt and blame emerge and we spend most of our lives apologising and weakening those walls of self -love; from this our boundaries become poor or non-existent; leaving us vulnerable to manipulative individuals.

With lack of boundaries and self -love, I didn't choose relationships they chose me; **anyone would do.**

I had no concept of what I deserved because my self- love was my seed for which no one had given me the full nutrients, the soil and water of love, knowledge and nurture.

I remember being hypnotised in the most severe part of my breakdown by a wonderful woman called Tessa; she had asked me a few questions about relationships; my body shook and a cold emotional pain shot through it. A sudden realisation that was hard to accept had entered my consciousness; **despite appearing very confident sexually for men I was an actress in an empty vessel.** I was trying desperately to attract and pour empty promises into my 'Father nurture' vacuum. The chasm from lack of self- love would leak straight back out again.

'There's a hole in my bucket,

Dear Liza, dear Liza,

There's a hole in my bucket,

Dear Liza, a hole.

Then mend it, dear Henry,

Dear Henry, dear Henry,

Then mend it, dear Henry,

Dear Henry, mend it.

With what shall I mend it,

Dear Liza, dear Liza?

With what shall I mend it,

Dear Liza, with what?

With straw,

Dear Henry, dear Henry, dear Henry,

With straw, dear Henry, dear Henry,

with straw….etc

Can we repair the bucket? Yes, to an extent by understanding how that hole got there and that we have plenty of solid buckets waiting to be filled with self-love. Occasionally we will observe ourselves using the damaged ones but it will be ok as we know we are not perfect and there are plenty of full ones. **It's not Liza's job or another person's job to look at the bucket, it's Henry's job.** In other words, it is you who ultimately fixes the problem by becoming aware of it.

When I was young, shortly after losing my Dad, I immersed myself in the life of the pub. It was exciting to get ready with my friend Tracey on a Friday. I had money I had stolen from my Dad whilst he was drunk. As I said in the last chapter, my theft felt like a payback for all the shit he was causing. It was my dream to fall in love and get rescued and have that man put his arm around me and protect me in some sort of normality. The TV, the adverts and films always show us that too; that this is the answer to our insecurities finding Mr or Mrs Right.

It was lucky really that I didn't get pregnant and I did find my way to University, because that was a middle class expectation in our house. I am so grateful that this was an expectation because it got me out of perpetuating the same pattern with another alcoholic in the little town where I was born.

Going to University opened my mind and opportunities for travelling which in turn gave me a passion for humanitarian causes. It didn't change my binge drinking but it was in a more 'interesting' atmosphere rather than a small town pub lounge.

My Mom and Dad were both kind people in normal circumstances so I think that came through in my philanthropic interests.

The other side to my positive endeavours was a wish to rescue, and yes it was the old cliché *'whilst rescuing others I was really trying to rescue myself.'*

I was lucky that none of the men I have been with were violent because the potential to choose an abusive relationship was high because of my desperate need to be loved 'safely' by a male. A paradox of our human condition; **in seeking safety, my vulnerability put me in potential danger.**

Yet I did get into a lovely relationship quite soon in University at Sheffield with a popular climbing dude. I was over the moon that he chose me; outwardly loud and confident as I was, everyone thought we were a lovely couple and he genuinely loved me. I can honestly say when he called the relationship off because I was going travelling, he broke my heart.

Despite being an attractive female, how I really felt inside was quite the opposite to the loud outgoing blonde, often drunk, I presented to the world.

This is how I really felt; *He was incredibly good looking and confident and I just can't believe he wanted me?*

I'm sure he was with me because he felt he had to be; there were plenty of girls buzzing around him and I was constantly trying to make best friends with them so there was no chance of them chatting him up. I was so anxious about this.

There was nothing, nothing about me that was attractive, I looked ok but on a wholesome level I was not worthy and I was faking it; someone would soon find out, but, when I was drunk, I didn't care.

I tried so hard to make all his friends like me that some of them thought I was an asshole. This devastated me. I probably was an asshole when I was drunk. I had so much confusion about who I was and what I had to offer I tried way too hard.

These thoughts were so locked into me they perpetuated into my being and would occupy my thoughts. Steve often said I wasn't in the moment with him. I could never tell him what was torturing me and I dreaded the inevitable which was that one day he would finish with me.

When this happened, my drinking hit hard again easing these vacuums. Steve was everything that my Dad was not.

Other relationships I formed could be controlling or narcissistic. My Dad wasn't narcissistic, I think he was in pain but generally narcissistic people are available when they are available on their terms and you revolve around their world. Does this sound familiar? My Father was not available and when he was it was on his terms; mostly drunk.

I would always revolve around my partner's worlds. I would have interests myself and appear independent but boyfriends were my world; positive or negative a life line, I needed to temporarily fill the massive chasm in my life; it was always temporary. I would never speak about my Dad's death, only when I was really drunk, and it wouldn't occur to me that this vacuum was so big it was a ticking time bomb. My outer shell, as shiny as it was, was thin and would one day be broken.

The unhelpful tools I used to soften the vacuum were alcohol, cigarettes and sometimes illegal drugs. The alcohol particularly was a problem I didn't even see this as I was at University and it just seemed normal to get totally trashed every time you went to the pub. I didn't drink every night but I was dependent. I am definitely less reliant on alcohol now but I have never completely abstained except when I was carrying my son and when I had a breakdown.

Cigarettes are long gone way before Seb came along, but I can't really have alcohol in the house; I wouldn't be drawn to it every night but, if I opened a bottle of wine, it would be drunk.

Alcohol is a major problem for a lot of people, it anesthetizes us from our pain but unfortunately the next day we have to face more physical and emotional pain. My hangovers come in the form of anxiety if I use alcohol excessively.

Knowing what I know now and why I am drawn to alcohol even though it caused destructive patterns in my house, gives me an ability to view the addiction and understand this and this is what I explain in the next chapter.

A lot of the psychiatrists based my breakdown on the trauma I experienced finding my Dad that morning, but when I started to explore, the damage was already emerging from an empty space at the dinner table and learning to not have my Dad there. When he was there it was generally in a destructive and chaotic way. These all had major consequences on me as a young girl and woman coming into the world.

Now follow your relationship patterns; if you are happy then why question them? If you have been drawn to control and manipulation, there is a way out through you.

Life in the red brick house lacked nurture even from my Mom who desperately loved me but was locked into trying to keep a dysfunctional ship afloat. I was running my own life. I can't believe that I have never been obese but can you see that in this house food was constantly accessible *so to compensate for lack of emotional support I used food.*

Food Vacuum

Food is something I have used to help me feel better emotionally, but of course it is short lived. It helps me understand why I get so hungry at night.

Waiting for my Dad to come home was stressful; how would he be? A happy drunk, an angry drunk? Would my Mom start shouting at him? Would he fall over and kill himself? Perhaps I should run a bath ready? If he got in the bath, I could steal his money from his back pocket and then help him into his pyjamas and he may just go to sleep?

I know, while I'm waiting for him I'll have a piece of toast, I'll get the box of broken biscuits out the cupboard to stop the churning in my solar plexus. My mind was too busy with questions, perhaps why I have always been an over thinker, always looking for answers, looking for control as there was none in the house at night. **There is none when your carer is drunk.** Food compensated the worry and loss I was experiencing.

Some people have a lack of food so their **food vacuum** becomes their obsession so they squirrel or steal food to fill the vacuum of scarcity.

Food and eating are massive especially in the U.K. **It must be crazy for countries of scarcity to wonder why we would be so unhappy when we have an abundance of food**, friends, safety and opportunity.

Food has become our compensation for the lack of understanding of ourselves and the disembodiment of our souls and communities which does not align itself with the natural world.

Most hunger pains are based often on an emotional lack rather than a need to eat. Yes, there are thyroid issues, yes there are people who put weight on more easily but they are all part of an unhealthy emotional state, disconnection from our natural source and a misunderstanding of our patterns, yarns and journeys we have taken. So the thing is ...

Learn about you, forgive you, observe you, love you, meditate, exercise reward yourself with things other than FOOD because you are filling another empty vacuum. (see self- love at the end of this chapter).

Health Vacuum

I'm still working at this one; my family and friends will tell you this, and that is ok. **When I wrote this book, I didn't write it from a place of perfection** but a miraculous journey of survival but guess what? I'm still working on me and I'm ok with that because I have some love most of the time for me. I sleep, I work, I'm kind, I love, I nurture but I also sometimes overeat, drink too much, get anxious about dying and leaving my son, then berate myself; I'm not perfect.

Imagine one day your Dad is there, and the next day he is dead and you discover him hard as a rock, rigor mortis set in. How will that affect you?

I'm sure people in war torn countries who have seen many of their families killed are numb to this but return them to a normal safe life and the psychological damage will appear.

After my Dad died, if I got a headache I thought it was a tumour or a potential brain haemorrhage, If I got palpitations I was sure it was a heart attack. I once went for an ECG with pains all down my arms when I was 16, as well as sleepless nights no one was telling me it was bereavement/ health anxiety. I mean who even acknowledged anxiety in the 1980s?

I used to drink; that was my anaesthetist to take the worry and pain away. What I was presenting to the world was happy go lucky blonde chick. I was this too, but there was a massive unconscious base of thought that life was short and any ailments probably led to death. There was no in between.

It is still there now sometimes and I am still healing this, there is no in between stage it goes from healthy happy to terminal/ dead catastrophic thoughts but I am aware of this pattern and I observe it. I sit to the side of it and my self -love takes over and soothes and calms.

She says "You remember you felt like this before and it was all ok; it didn't last. You've been triggered again by lack of sleep, too much alcohol, seeing such and such.' So the acceptance and nurture begins.

I genuinely did make myself ill in my late 20s, I was working and playing hard as a recycling collector in Bristol; eco chick, rebel rebelling, fighting for the planet. I got glandular fever and following this had bouts of chronic fatigue.

Through research I found phyto nutrients (see Ambrotose also used for Fibromyalgia amongst other nutrients) and that is why I can confidently write a 'nutrients for mental health chapter,' I have been there and researched and spent a lot of money on supplements; some useful and some not.

I have gone and often do from total health freak to a drunken bum; one extreme to another, but both states are levelling off gently as I come to accept me for me every day.

I was too ill to go near alcohol when I was in breakdown. During this time, I found myself in a cage worse than death. Surviving that cage has made me on the whole 'not give a shit' about dying. It appeared to release me from this burden but traces still appear and **I accept them.** Sometimes I find myself researching miracle cures and intently looking at different detox or health diets. This has both good sides and bad and I balance both.

Meditation helps with this, it make me feel safe; listening to Deepak Chopra and Eckhart Tolle (see Chapter 9) calm my sometimes anxious thoughts. Most importantly what helps is observing my vacuums like a Mother to a child; a skill I continue to develop. I calm the child and reason with her.

On the whole I am happy but aware of all my peculiarities; understandable peculiarities and I'm just fine with them; my half repaired buckets; my vacuums.

The anxiety does not belong to me, the breakdown does not either but the vacuums are mine to accept and nurture and this in itself will heal their holes.

Nurture Vacuum

Let's talk about nurture in general because the Father nurture Vacuum, and Mother nurture Vacuum ARE MASSIVE ...lack of nurture can lead us away from an amazing journey of self -love. With all my heart I hope this book guides you back to the tools you have had inside you since you were born, that perhaps your parents were unable to teach you or a trauma stripped from you.

Later on, I was to carry these vacuums into my life; over privileged with travel and opportunity but unaware and unresolved emotional vacuums that can in later life destroy us.

If you have had total hardship, the same can be true, or you become aware more quickly about emotional intelligence. Each person is individual and have their own paths to explore and understand.

I would say from this experience I have learned that exploring ourselves, no matter how advanced you think you may be, is a life long journey. At the same time as understanding your journey know you **are not defined by it and are connected to an infinite source of possibility.** Particularly with hardship and 'lack ofs' this persona we carry prevents you from falling and holding the identity of a victim which in effect just perpetuates the identity in a vicious circle.

Understanding is the key. Remember you are not your trauma.

The end result of recovery is always an ability to be empathic, kind and explorative of human beings, but most of all honour your vacuums and once you know and are aware of them and are prepared to accept them, they no longer stay as our vacuums we can then view them as **just our inner children tugging at our sleeves**, till we stop and note their fears so they feel heard and do not have to be destructive.

It got me into a lot of trouble when I didn't understand the jigsaw of my life and the vacuums that were holding me back, and of course I'm far from perfect now either, but by understanding where I came from and the vacuums I developed (not purposefully), it gives me the ability to re-nurture them and dissolve their power.

Do you recognise any of these vacuums in your life? The other ones of course are the

Mother Vacuums (similar to the Father Vacuum)

Loss or lack of a Mother can cause untold issues for males and females. In the same way the Father can but loss of Mother or Mother being absent through addiction can also create untold anger of being let down.

The Mother is the ultimate creator of life and nurturer, she is the essence and platform of our emotional development. My Father never got over his Mother's death and so absolved his pain continually with alcohol and cigarettes that ultimately killed him.

These vacuums are so powerful that I have experienced adults operating at the exact emotional age as when a trauma, separation, an absence or bereavement took place with that child. It is fascinating as often they operate as fully functional adults but their emotional capacities are blunted, limited and underdeveloped. They are vulnerable to attracting the wrong person because their need to be Fathered or Mothered is so obviously 'out there' it makes them beacons to bringing controlling relationships into their lives.

Female and male stable energies are important in our development; **to know that you seek a Mother stops you from jumping into over controlling or domineering imbalanced relationships.** Resolving and making peace with our loss before we project it through another relationship will on the whole attract healthier relationships into our lives.

Material Vacuums

This is one most of us suffer from here in The West. Purely because of the fragmented materialistic culture we have developed: **our God has become consumerism.** If we feel low, let's do a binge shop; somehow having a bag full of things we 'need' will give us a short term buzz and soothe the inner discontent but sadly like any addiction, it is short lived.

Don't feel bad about having a shop or enjoying yourself, just be conscious of why you are doing it and evolve yourself back into the planetary consciousness.

The most rewarding action that will last for a long time **is giving**. We are natural givers but **our culture over the last three decades has taught us to grab as much as we can for ourselves. It is an unfulfilled vacuum.** Some of the happiest and most satisfied people are those who give up materialism and surrender to giving.

Breaking the shame cycle

So, with the vacuums in mind and let's put all the negativity into one outcome; **low self -esteem or self- worth**. Without even realising my whole being was flooded with both of these before my breakdown. As I have repeated many times, **I relied on the** outside world to form and judge me whereas now through surviving such an extreme time, as well as all the methods I show you in this book, my opinion comes from me a place of SELF LOVE.

It is not an egotistic or narcissistic love, more a solid inner foundation of faith in me and an ability to nurture those insecurities. The adult parent is now strong enough to tell my inner child that she is good enough. Here is a practical example...

I write a lot of poetry. It's definitely not Kay Tempest and I'm not under any illusion that it's, genius but it's a creation that improves and manifests and I love embracing it.

Since recovering I often share it with people. I do it because I'm expressing a feeling they may connect to. Often a few people press 'like' and comment on; occasionally I get a negative reaction.

Firstly, before my breakdown I wouldn't have even shared my poetry yet alone cope with a negative response so let's look at that as an example;

Someone in person or on social media says;

"What are those poems you are writing, were you drunk?

Really they're not good I think you need to look at another hobby, (ha ha, LOL etc)." So passive aggressive now they've turned it into a joke,

So, before the breakdown my first response would have been I would have felt sick ,I would have felt very hot. My inner self **which is my inner child** would have felt ashamed for being so stupid; of course they're bad/ what did you expect?

It would have bothered me for weeks and I wouldn't have put any of my work out now. **That person's opinion would have defined me.** My inner child would have been reassured that this was the right way. 'Your poetry is rubbish don't put it out there again...what were you thinking?' Done. The feeling of sickness would have eventually subsided.

What happens now is a dialogue between my adult self and my inner child; yes, it is a conversation with me (bear with me), it goes like this.

Adult "Hey I know you're upset about this, It's ok to be upset you know!"

Adult "We know from your vacuums it is easy for you to feel this way quite quickly."

Child Silence.

Adult "Remind me again why you like writing?"

Child "It helps express how I feel."

Adult "Well that's good."

Child "Yep I guess."

Silence, take a deep breath.

Adult "So why do you like to share those words?"

Child "Because it might help other people."

Adult "Wow that's a good thing too."

Child "Yes."

Adult "Have you had any positive responses from them?"

Child "Yes, actually quite a few."

Adult "So actually whilst you're not really looking for praise or to boost your ego here, although I guess it's good to have those positive response, but is that why you do it?"

Child "No I don't think so."

Adult "I'm thinking that by maybe helping people you're trying to create connection?"

Child "Yes definitely that is definitely what I'm trying to achieve."

Adult "So does it matter if a person chose to be negative about it?"

Child "I guess not."

Adult "Let's look at the person that reacted like that. Why do you think they may have done that?"

Child "They genuinely thought my poem was shit!" (starts to get upset)

Adult "Can you accept that not everyone likes everything you do even though the objective of what you are doing is positive?"

Child "I suppose so!"

Adult "Is there any other reason other than he just doesn't like your work that he would choose to sort of be …well let's be honest he was being mean, right?"

Child "yes he was being mean…perhaps he isn't happy."

Adult "If his motive was not to help and just to be mean…perhaps he is not happy perhaps he is projecting that on you?"

Child "Yes I think so."

Adult "I'm very proud that you have come so far."

Child "Thank you"

Adult "I'm also proud that you wouldn't let anyone's negativity stop you from sharing your feelings with people in order to try and help them."

Child' Thanks, that makes me feel much better."

So we've healed, we've calmed, we've praised , we've motivated; this is your inner strength. It really is like talking to your children in a non-shameful way. If your child had been berated at football you would say "do you love the football? You can't be great straight away you have to give it time...don't let someone else stop your passion"...etc.

You can apply this to anything you do, it is your internal approval of you. Understanding why you might take a self-destructive path, understanding your vacuums is the first step and once you put the above method into practice. It is a way of calming and healing before things get out of hand. Don't let the negative thoughts fester; have the conversation.

Other help to resolve your Vacuums and the teachers that will guide you.

I've already said that feeling your pain and allowing it once you are aware of the inner turmoil will stop you putting energy into these vacuums and I showed a practical example of breaking the 'shame cycle' above. There are also some phenomenal teachers who explain and guide you through this process that I would highly recommend. Listen to podcasts and read their books, whatever works,(see Chapter 8 and references section.)

Finally, I want to say this; you may have noticed I haven't referred to any one particular therapy but:

 If you are lucky enough to afford therapy or find a decent therapist **all of them in some way rely on observation of yourself**. That observation will come from an empathic or nurturing voice. So, CBT will observe and ask your thought processes such things as "What is this thought I am having, is it relevant or realistic; is it likely to happen?" This ,in effect, will slow the process of catastrophizing/ spiralling thoughts and each time it comes back you will ask the same relevant questions till the thought just stops holding that power.

Thoughts are not you, they are thoughts so having negative ones need to be challenged/ observed so you can change them.

Mindfulness will make you understand that a thought is simply a thought; observe it let it pass and be aware/ conscious of your immediate surroundings or the present (see 'The Power Of Now' Eckhart Tolle.)

These therapies didn't work for me when I was in acute anxiety as it seemed so physical, although they are helpful now.

Hypnotherapy will access patterns and memories from your unconscious so you can understand and change the negative mechanical reactions your body produces from them.

Interpersonal therapies will look at your relationship with others but will still ask you to observe your responses.

So, in effect we are all looking for patterns, like solving a riddle but we are all looking to be able to soothe and dissolve these patterns through self- nurture and ultimately self- love.

Can you learn to self- love through these techniques in this chapter? I think you can, especially if you read Chapter 8 and understand the great teachers that state 'Our past is not us." Once we understand how our past has defined us then we can un-define us by simply observing these chinks and nurturing them.

Nurture, nurture, nurture and acceptance! This does not mean you can't use good patterns from the past or forget your past completely. It is not forgetting who you are but locking into another source beyond all the thoughts that you have filled your head with.

Such thoughts are good to understand but do not pollute us so we become so toxic that our ability to appreciate and be in the present moment becomes impossible.

When you are clear about these patterns you can use a thought in a positive way to create incredible outcomes instead of self-sabotaging habits that lead you into rabbit holes.

Remember though, if you are highly anxious right now then safety and stability are your priority before you go into the jigsaws, the vacuums, spirituality and nutrition.

I want to share this next poem with you after these chapters about relationships. This was a beautiful relationship I had with a free spirit boat builder from Falmouth. He built his own boat and had sailed it across to the Caribbean alone. His boat was a small fibre glass yacht called Splinter. He became ill in the Caribbean and had to return home to recover and work. He met me during this time. I was still wobbly and on meds but together we discovered a beautiful world of drinking in Falmouth bars and hanging about on a boat he rented. It was quite magical that my brain had started to understand enjoyment again and he introduced me to Spotify which in turn returned the magic of music to my life (see also Cold Hands). My friends thought he was more in love with me than I him as I had my heart broken by someone just before him., who I went out with early on in my recovery. However, when T returned to the Caribbean to collect and sail back Splinter he discovered that he was not a settling down man and the sea was his home. I did miss him for a while after but accepted that our time together was exactly what it was supposed to be. Some relationships just aren't supposed to be forever.

Last hotel trip before T went off to fly to the Caribbean to collect his little boat Splinter (April 2017).

Love after breakdown

I miss you

In the cabin

Where you lived floating

Me ...Recovering

And scared

While you so doting

you asked, 'What is anxiety?'

so interested

 I knew

You wouldn't understand

But you did

And then you listened

As I recall nervously first hand.

Still but wobbling

Glinting

Masts creeking and squabbling

Over kissing the stars.

Fresh from head prison

under bright little eyes

I'm coming home; an alien from Mars

Sensing, soothing

More certain days

Loved up

Skating to chic Falmouth bars

Smells of old books

Walking home in a haze

Through our tapestry of tales

We rethread our hurts

We have time to trace from beginning to end

From the finish to start

But somewhere In the Caribbean

A little Splinter has your heart

Happy, protected

Nothing but hope

A beautiful life

floating

Held by a rope!

Back to the magic realm

Of cabin beds

And Spotify

Lyrics and dreams

Laid out at the helm

Touching each string of my heart

With Release and learning

Time to chat

Lost in Desert Discs

You always loved that!

Then for more coffee

Brewed by the Kimble

Ground like love potion

And listen so well

Never ready for this solid life

No sign or symbol

With your love

Gone

Swallowed by ocean!

Chapter 7a

An exercise for physical and mental trauma including PTSD

The Story of Jen; The story of many.

I recently put in this exercise about physical trauma. I was thinking about it during a walk and the next day serendipity played her card; I met an amazing woman in my wild swimming place who had managed to flee her abusive ex husband.

It was severe abuse and luckily the Police had responded well and given the abuser a strict zone exclusion whilst they waited to be sentenced which kept her feeling relatively secure but still traumatised and partially scared.

How had they taken her claims seriously? Many abuse cases they get locked up with 'he said she said,' manipulations and *this is often the the best skill an abuser has.* So it is hard to untangle the truth.

Let's call her Jenny; she had no confidence still shaken up but pleased she had done the best thing for her children. Her children knew instinctively that she was being abused and her soul taken; a lot of it as behind closed doors. Her son had said .. *"Mommy when your heart hurts mine does too."*

Beautiful words from children like this don't need explaining do they..children have this way.

During our conversation we were both at times getting teary. I found her amazing and she didn't understand the bravery she had used to get out of the situation because her own power was still seeped in fear and trauma; she was in recovery.

Jenny who felt helpless found a glimmer of light when she discovered an ap for just £9.99 (the best £ 9.99 she had ever spent!) probably created by an amazing person who understood this type of hidden abuse and control over another human. The ap sensed motion and secretly film abusive situations. She managed to film three severe attacks and rape without him knowing. Then she fled. I praised her ingenuity to even think of this and the fact the universe responded with an exact fit of hat she needed. This tiny human being who as being controlled by a monster and she had managed to take herself to safety with strong evidence in her pocket..

I tried to explain the thoughts I was having about methods to help recovery from physical trauma or any trauma really buit when someone has infiltrated and controlled your body you may feel any of these..**dirty, disgusting, powerless, infiltrated, stupid, ashamed, not worthy, out of control, weak, contaminated**... The list is endless but here are the scientific facts that may help think about it differently;

'*About 330 billion cells are replaced daily, equivalent to about 1 percent of all our cells. In 80 to 100 days, 30 trillion will have replenished—the equivalent of a new you.*'

(scientific america.com)

Telling yourself this every day in meditation and repeating that your cells are renewing and becoming new from the trauma can be helpful. This is known as a **mantra** *a voice of intent; you are creating a* **'new you'** *and we can enhance that thought by making the intent visible by using very powerful Reiki symbols; an old energy healing system. A Reiki wheel is not only visible it ill put the bad energy that has absorbed into your body and sending it back to its source.*

This sounds like witch craft to some but is is not. Humans have used words and symbols for centuries to utilize energy. Energy systems and auras have been a huge part of ancient healing.

You are not wishing bad on anybody all you are doing is sending the energy someone has put into to you back to them because they are the source of the trauma the responsibility of that trauma should not lie in your body; the abuser has to pick it up. It may be that it will get sent back in a form of healing but that is not your worry.

Ask any healer or Reiki master how powerful this can be. Even if it wasn't (which it is) **you are focusing that trauma outside of your body it is no longer within you and now you are shifting it so it is not part of you.**

With PTSD notof a person but an experience this method can still be used; you are sending the energy back to the place. If you have been in a war for example this energy then may be useful to create peace. Again this is not your concern but the words on paper can take the trauma metaphorically out of your body.

Here is a simple phrase to create and then look at the illustrations and it will show you how to draw a wheel to send energy to the situation. Everyday ,even at night which can be calming place your hand over this piece of paper and feel the heat from your hand send your natural power into healing.

Here is the simple phrase.

'THIS TRAUMA IS NOT MINE I RETURN IT TO ITS SOURCE.'

1. The words

2.draw the wheel clockwise over the the words.

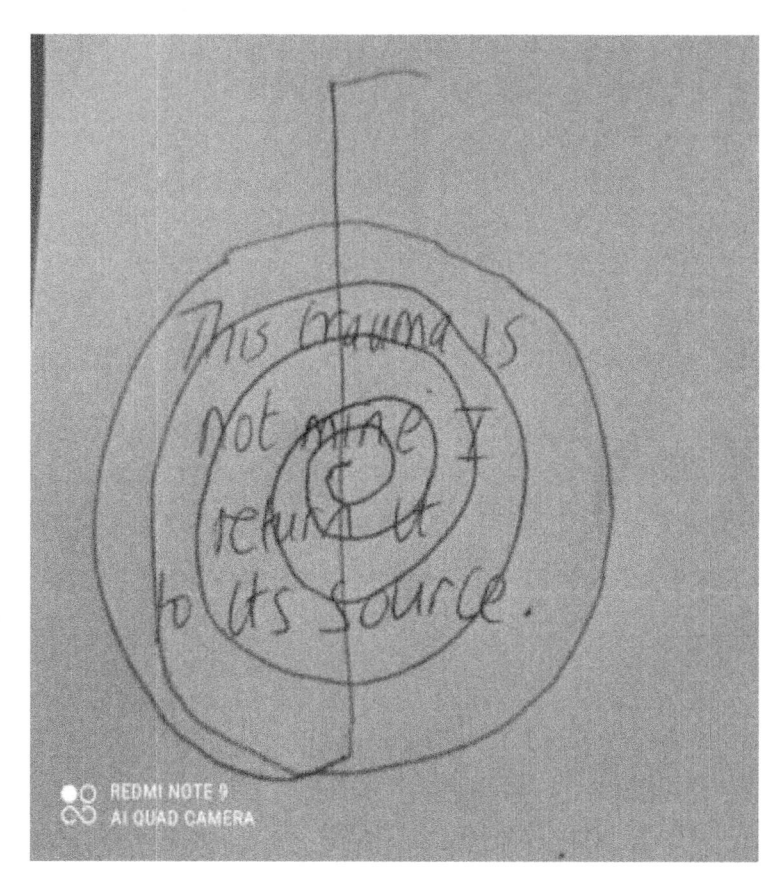

3. Finished..this is your power the trauma lies on the table not in your body and your cells are renewing you all the time.

If you are experiencing full blown ptsd you may need to stabilize before you do it but the regularity of this exercise will create healing.

Remember You are not your trauma. *You are not your past..Namaste!*

Chapter 8

Self -Love and Healing; The spiritual way to help recovery and renewal.

These paths as well as great people have helped me during my recovery. In my state and level of anxiety I couldn't read, so don't think you have failed if you cannot absorb this right now because you are in a vulnerable or highly anxious state. These ideas and tools are the people that will guide you through recovery.

Self- love, meditation and guided work

Brooke Castillo

I want to tell you about a woman called Brooke Castillo who wrote; 'How come if I'm so smart I can't lose weight?' Yes, what a long title, but her work focuses on us understanding our thought, feeling action cycle, which we can put into any aspects of our life. The equation is simple:

Our thoughts create our feelings which drive our actions.

Now look at that sentence above and realise how our initial thoughts lead to a manifestation of what we want or who we are.

You can put this into any part of life. Brooke's first work was coaching with weight then she expanded to other aspects of life and her work touches on many parts of life. Her podcasts are truly inspiring; they empower and give hope.

Brooke bases her weight philosophy on the idea that we don't allow ourselves to understand what is real hunger and what is just a feeling. Try it! If you have Spotify or YouTube look at 'The Life Coach' sessions.

Brooke takes us through her own journey of manifestation and she touches base with some spiritual teachers. Some of her work involves manifestation of material wealth; I'm still not so comfortable with this and she would say to me now "it's because I don't think I'm worth it.' etc.

My material wealth isn't great at the moment but my gratitude I feel every day for surviving such a gruesome journey makes me feel that, whilst I would like more money, this is not my journey or my awakening, and the money will come later but the connecting to universal consciousness and helping others is my first port of call.

Brooke's work and podcasts are amazing and I listened to her avidly during my recovery. Some of the work she has done with setting and understanding boundaries has been really useful to me as, remember from my background, having an alcoholic or an addicted parent can make our boundaries blurred and weak.

So, back to the vacuums from the last chapter, let's just recap; when you discover your Vacuum, learn to love it first it's just a chink that makes you unique. To balance it, observe it, nurture it and calm it.

Meditation and teachings from the likes of Deepak Chopra, Eckhart Tolle and Joe Dispenza reflect this healing and are now great comfort to me. I want to share some of their wisdoms in case they become useful to you or indeed already are. It might be that you will find your own voice who help you heal in time. The following are some of my favourites:

Deepak Chopra and Joe Dispenza

(I put these two guys together because some of their ideas interlink/ bear with me.)

The voice of Deepak Chopra in his meditations is both calming and nurturing, he gets you to connect back to your higher self and human consciousness which opens our souls to abundance. Now if someone told me this when I was ill, I may have wanted to kill them.

I couldn't concentrate, I was exhausted and the thought of contemplating a 'higher self' or 'universal abundance' was so un-reachable.

On recovery, however, his daily meditation practice is vital to me; they are also free. He has Abundance meditations, Hope meditations, Health Meditations amongst others. He is highly positive about our future and gives a mind-blowing perspective of how powerful we are as human beings.

Whilst understanding our journeys and vacuums, spiritual teachers such as Chopra and also Eckhart Tolle make us realise **our life stories are not entirely us and we should not be controlled by them.** They are partially a story of the ego; our tool to control our mind which desperately tries not to lose control but often serves little purpose in our development.

The ego wants answers immediately and when it doesn't get what it wants it becomes anxious. The ego has it uses, but as a master of our mind it is destructive. The ego as Chopra points out many times **'thrives on lack'**…..it always wants MORE: more money, more time in order to reach the final goal of happiness it is a futile journey because the **contentment is never there but in this moment which is the gift we call life.**

As Master Oogway in Kung Fu Panda classically illustrates in his famous words:

'***Yesterday is history. Tomorrow is a mystery, but today is a gift!*** *That is why it is called the present.*'

Connecting beyond the ego to universal consciousness leads to unlimited opportunities even in times of uncertainty in fact Deepak says;

"Watch opportunity spring from the fountain of uncertainty."

For me someone who has suffered with health anxiety.... Chopra's words are soothing as well as other influential books such as Evolve the Brain (Joe Dispenza/ see references) all these great teachers show evidence genetics given to us by our parents are only a small part of the picture of our health outcomes.

Both Chopra and Joe Dispenza present scientific research that makes us understand that beyond genetics there are so many actions habits and training such as meditation that can have a significant positive effect on our health and well- being.

Chopra connects very much with science on a spiritual level and if you feel that science has become too distorted and corrupt some of Deepak's interviews convey the opposite and give us hope about just what miracles we are as human beings. He has taken part in scientific studies attached to age and renewal of the body. **We are 95% microbiome** which means basically bacteria. So, the food we put in our bodies without hormones, without petroleum, without antibiotics are an important enrichment to these incredible systems.

Only 25000 out of millions of our genetic makeup is influenced by our parent's genes and these can be reprogrammed or turned off with lifestyle and stress and it is the **microbiome 'super highway'** as Deepak calls this that influences our genetic changes. We learn then that lifestyle, exercise and meditation to still the mind calm the voice or chatter of the ego and of course provide the right fuel or nutrients for this to happen.

Although great sages have known this through centuries, ideas using terms such as 'the elasticity of the brain' in Jo Dispenza's book ' Evolve the Brain' are relatively new. Such philosophies provide us with hopeful concepts that our health is not fixed and we have the power to reverse even extreme health problems and change the very patterns in our brain that create them. Look at Joe Dispenza's meditations and self- hypnosis sessions on you tube;

they are powerful and hopeful. Dr. Joe Dispenza Meditation || How To DEFEAT Anxiety And Live In BLISS - Bing video

https://www.bing.com/videos/search?q=jo+dispenza+anxiety+meditaion&ru=%2fvideos%2fsearch%3fq%3djo%2520dispenza

Most viruses and cancers start in the body as inflammation and these can be renewed and influenced by less chemicals in our food, organic plant- based food, healthy fats, and low sugar diets. These not only fuel our body but as you will see In chapter nine they change the way we view the world. Meditation then further reduces stress at significant levels.

Here are some of the ideas Deepak conveys in interviews and meditation that may inspire or influence you to access their teachings;

- We are all connected to an incredible abundant source more powerful than any institution or oppressor; this ultimately empowers us.
- The brain communicates to 50 trillion cells; Disconnection from our bodies and ignoring these signals means we can fall into poor life style choices. **Give nourishing signals get nourishing positive response. When your mind meditates so does your body.**
- Unlimited and eternal we can use conscious intention to manifest dreams, create abundance.
- Mind matter and spirit work in conjunction with one another to manifest abundance;' *in the silent field of all possibilities dwell the seeds of success.*' Live from within desires manifest easily.
- Continual relentless effort is often required to achieve in the three -dimensional world; but tapping into your unconscious can manifest dreams and is not luck but **living in alignment with the source/ spirit**. Once connected we can enjoy everyday miracles.

- Perhaps you are an accountant but want to be an artist? Focus on your feelings and body when you imagine this dream. Align your body with spirit and make those creative choices which bring you closer to your desires.
- Meditation can help let go of these negative trains of thought that feed the ego and tap into this source of possibilities.
- GO within to that place of inner quiet experiencing connection with higher self.
- From uncertainty springs the fountain of possibilities.
- Bodies flourish with constant exchange from the universe. Nature perfect symphony.
- **Nowhere in the natural world does hoarding exist; giving and receiving is part of nature's gift.** If you want joy give joy to others; circulate the flow of abundance by helping others get what they want. Silently bless everyone for all the good things they have in their life. Give and you shall receive.
- Remain open when all gifts are offered to you.
- Choices you make should nourish you and others; in other words, **Karma conscious choice making**. Taking proper care of a child, using earth's resources responsibly'. Every action creates a force of energy that is returned to us.
- Unbounded joy limitless love, greater material possessions.
- 'Some look at our physical world and see lack others abundance. Others feel limited based on certain messages they have received in the past.'
- We believe matter to be reality and often view as changeless yet matter and form continually change so what then is reality?

As we exist in the physical plane, we live in the level of the mind which sees things and evaluates...**the mind is potential energy so we can change our physical world by changing our thoughts and beliefs beyond the mind resides the spirit**; eternal unchanging imbued with pure limitless potential that enables us to manifest miracles. The world is a construct of our own interpretations.

Whilst you are reading these ideas they are making you feel a certain way; I have no doubt it is positive: and that is the whole point by accessing our inner self we create a whole new dialogue of who we are; ironically the dialogue comes from a silence.

At the end of meditation, we always say **'Namaste' and for those who don't know what it means it is "I honour the light in you."** Think about the love and respect you are sharing with another human. This is meditation; this is the path to self- love.

Eckhart Tolle

Eckhart Tolle is humorous, mesmerising and calming. He had an epiphany in his late 20s when contemplating suicide after many years of suffering he connected with his true consciousness and became fearless and content.

His descriptions of anxiety (see link below) are so accurate that you know he understands. He describes the ongoing thought patterns that create the uncomfortable feeling in the solar plexus; in other words, the negative thought pattern eventually forces the brain to think. it feels like a real situation so prepares the body to run or fight (*fight or flight.*)

'Because my body can't tell the difference between the thoughts and the reality of what is happening.'

Interestingly, I never felt this was my description of what happened to me. I always felt the physical feeling came first followed by the negative thought patterns. To my joy Eckhart describes this in the video right at the end.

I was really pleased to hear someone recognising this. It made me understand why mindfulness at the time seemed unhelpful to me because the start of my pain was at my physical core. Eckhart describes this as *'pain body'* so trauma or PTSD being at the heart of this reaction. This really makes us understand why sometimes this can 'just happen' rather than build up over months or years.

This sudden feeling is also described at the beginning and in Chapter nine when it describes mechanical reactions in the brain between the Hippocampus and Amygdala.

Either way both are treatable by all the methods I have described. Most importantly I want you to know that this is why not all therapies may appear to work or be right for you at that time of your journey as this terrifying cloud descends on you.

Eckhart recommends **separating yourself from the thoughts**; which is right, but he may seem like he is being unsympathetic if you are in an anxious state now, but please listen to the whole video because what you get is a man who totally understands what this illness is doing to you and remember he has experienced it and transcended completely from it.

https://www.bing.com/videos/search?q=eckhart+tolle+anxiety+and+fear&&view=detail&mid=04530D413C3FF8A5B29E04530

Like Chopra his words are not weighed by money but accessible and mostly free to all. His intentions are pure and invigorate many lives. He speaks slowly and holds silence well in a room allowing a calmness to prevail.

In an increasingly restless world Tolle provides serenity with notions such **'even a dying forest has decaying matter that will feed a whole new growth'**.

We are all one being manifesting through countless forms of life; connection to our source and other is imperative for happiness.

Tolle reflects as I have already observed from poor mental health is that our systems and societies reflect our consciousness and, currently, we are in a profit not people lead world which creates fragmentation; our governments reflect the consciousness we have become.

Tolle teaches how healing can be sought from understanding our egoic mind and not be run by its continual fears and wants as it relies on 'lack of' (like the empty vacuums I described.) Pain and negativity can become part of the egoic response.

We all carry energetic traces of pain and suffering that can become part of our state. This goes back to my learning of how to observe the anxiety, acknowledge it and letting it move on. Sometimes it requires nurture but **fundamentally a separation of the voice that is calling the shots in a desperate attempt to reach happiness.**

Tolle says *happiness is outside of the ego mind and here in the present.* When we connect with this magnificent moment then there are no demands because we are just that and there is no fear.

What is interesting when we think of states of addiction is Eckhart Tolle's talks about them as an attempt for people to escape the constant chatter of the ego, an unconscious longing to be free of yourself.

Simple meditation techniques for a short time daily can create amazing results. I recently broke my leg and even though my body was in trauma and, despite a few tears throughout my stay in hospital and much pain, my pulse remained slow and my breathing deep and steady. This was not only because I had suffered a breakdown which has made me stronger it was also because I have learned and listened to meditation and thought processes through Chopra, Tolle and Dispenza amongst others.

As Tolle says 'you are more likely to realise and connect to your true consciousness in a prison cell rather than a private jet,' and that is hope, it is also profound ideas like this that Tolle comes out with totally unconsciously makes me immediately connect to them. Tolle never plans what he will say it feels like a natural flow and source of knowledge from his unconscious.

Here is a great interview with Tolle from **Russell Brand** another great spirit who has bridged so many gaps between spirituality and mainstream; and for that **Russell Brand** I thank you from the bottom of my heart!

https://www.youtube.com/watch?v=6EwzvKF-o_Y

Brand also bravely highlights the big flaws and gaps within our disconnected world. He interviews many spiritual people in a playful and engaging way. Also thank you Russell for making me laugh and as a true survivor I see you supporting the most vulnerable people in society. This is beyond your status and ego, it is your true self.

Chris Duncan

I want to talk about two more people who have really inspired me recently. Remember, meditation is great and then some further work involves really restructuring our deep patterns. The Vacuums in Chapter 6 covers this but then we can really start to uncover our inner make up with Chris Duncan's Work. Duncan's book 'You're Not Broken' talks about reconstructing our identity. Actually, it is not reconstructing our identity; it blows it out of the water.

Duncan looks at these patterns we have created from our parents and experiences and explains **'we are attached to our limitations'**.

This connects to both Tolle and Chopra's themes of 'we are not our past' and **we as humans are connected to infinite possibilities when we let go of ego constraints**

Whilst my Vacuum work covers awareness of our traits and lacks, Duncan actually goes one further by showing methods to 'recode' ourselves by addressing our **Superconscious.**

Our **Superconscious** is the essence of what we are it has no feelings but codes of our values, this then influences the **unconscious** which creates programmes and feelings that connect to our identity and goals in our **self- conscious.**

Duncan explains these systems in terms of energy and here is the interesting thing; these codes can carry through **seven generations.** This may explain that under hypnosis some people experience different experiences from past lives.

Einstein said *'All Matter is Energy'* so it doesn't seem an unreasonable idea that we carry these codes within ourselves as energy. So, then we can look at our development like this;

"As creative energy you will always take the path of least resistance. However, you created all resistance as a useful barrier in an attempt to avoid pain. If you experienced a negative outcome, your **superconscious** *would create a blockage to stop it from happening in the future. Think of it like putting a dam in the way of a stream. No flow can happen until the dam is opened. By* **recoding** *you open the dam."*

So, he describes different identity types which you may well recognise yourself in. Even as a 'high achiever' this identity still holds its limitations and this is where it gets interesting;

'For example, if you didn't get attention growing up expect for when you did something amazing, you may decide you are not worthy of love/ attention just the way you are and set up a structure to do amazing things to finally prove you are worthy. You will get really motivated and set a big goal and move towards it. However, as soon as you get close to achieving it, you will find a way to sabotage it.'

This is a setup. You don't achieve your goal because if you were to actually "make it," **you would have to accept you are worthy, and your former identity would be lost;** *you would no longer know who you are."* (35)

Does anyone recognise this pattern? I certainly did.

There are so many variations but for me the 'not worthy' was definitely part of my identity and that is understandable when I trace my journey. It really becomes a puzzle. Duncan's work is aimed at getting you out of a trap of chasing a 'moving goal post.' It opens us up as beings open to infinite possibilities.

So there are 'the victims, the 'lack ofs,' the 'not worthy,' and so on. The limited identities often overlap as well.

I was drawn to this work because I feel like when I experienced breakdown I broke something in me that was able to release some of my fears about 'being liked.'

This work is an affirmation of me moving on as an energetic source instead of a closed book limiting myself with lack of self-worth and seeking an ideal partner to bridge the gap.

It is perhaps work that can be done in recovery and a lot of Duncan's seminars are free.

Donna Eden

Finally, I want to mention some energetic methods you can use on yourself captured by Donna Eden in her work from 'The Eden Method' again some of the basic workshops are free. This is gentle enough work to do with your carer to try to release anxiety when you are in the midst.

Donna Eden is a gentle soul you can see and feel that when you watch her. She empowers us to understand our own fields of energy outside our body and recharge them in order to boost our immune systems, stop anxiety, make us feel safe and grounded again and many more.

Before I experienced breakdown I would have possibly laughed at this type of work as it just seems too 'gentle' to make a difference. Now I understand we all give out energy and even our thoughts have the power to diminish our fields of energy or enhance them when we are happy. Other human beings pick up on this. This is science and every quantum analysis reflects this.

Most people that find themselves in mental trauma have often denied their sensitivity and have taken on too much energetically, even form others, for a long time. Recognising you are sensitive is not a weakness. It can be a strength in the form of empathy and being able to help others; but only when you have fully formed the nurture and self- love needed otherwise your 'energy tank' is just filling others and leaving you empty. Self- love leaves the tank abundant.

Other human beings pick up on our energy so people in mental distress will have very low resistance and limited fields so it takes special kind of people to literally shine in their lives because it is hard work. That is why I have written practical methods.

Donna Eden could see all energy fields from when she was a child and she experienced these energy fields diminishing in people when others were cruel or hurtful. She says that *'If only we could all see what we do to someone else when we are mean.'*

The other interesting point about Eden is that she was chronically ill with MS from an early age. She had severe health problems and she learned to heal herself with the energy system she had been observing her whole life.

Most of the recommendations in this chapter are actually **people who have experienced real darkness in their lives and it was this that transformed them**; so, hold onto this when you are feeling lousy.

Getting involved in a community of a spiritual teacher's work may help you feel connected. If you feel safe, or even with your carer it can be a great distraction from your heavy heart to a lighter place. When recovered it may become part of your life. Here are some final ideas that you may want to carry in your daily routines and actions;

Try just to be!

A lot of the spiritual teachers convey the technique of learning 'to be' rather than do. Children have this natural ability to exist out of time frames to be fascinated and enamoured with life because they are 'being' and as parents we spend so much time to get our kids **'to do'** we have forgotten how to **'be'** with them. 'Do your homework!',' have you flushed the toilet?',' did you eat your dinner?'

They equally respond back with demands 'can I have this' etc, but if you become playful and creative most natural children will immediately respond to these invites outside of routine with great enthusiasm.

So, I have introduced you to some spiritual guiders that affirm all the lessons I learned during and after my breakdown and they can be very powerful sources to take you back to peace.

Finally: Trauma, your higher self and WAKING UP

With all these teachings in mind we can safely say;

You are not your trauma.

This is easier said than done because during that trauma whether during childhood or adult your body will have taken on an energetic field that has shaped you and your reactions for the rest of your life.

This is similar territory to The Vacuums chapter about bringing in a' third party' to draw upon and with meditation we can develop this. This third entity is called, in spiritual terms, our **'higher self'**.

Many spiritual teachers refer this as 'our light' and source.' In other words, our true selves, and it is this through connecting with our unconscious we learn to listen to. So next time you are aware you might be going into conflict or fear try and connect with your higher self. What you will notice is the higher self does not react emotionally it observes and will react in the best way for the higher good.

So, you may be going through this mental pain because actually you are clearing energy becoming more compassionate as a soul and you will come out of this shining. So, hold on.

I was listening to a podcast the other day by a spiritual teacher and, as she was talking, I felt I was in a meditative state. Bear in mind where we are in the world now (2021) with a 'Pandemic' and a world full of fear. This was the message that came through and this message will end this chapter...

'Over the next few months years some of us are **waking up** to the fact that the very institutions that claimed to keep us safe have in fact done the opposite. Through fear it has created dis ease, dis harmony and divide of the human spirit that has literally made us **forget who we are.** Once we have grieved over the deception our lights and power will shine and you are reading this my friend through suffering because you are part of the light. Hold on too my dear friend the sun will rise again!'

Cold Hands; the start of recovery

Musicians and artists

Noted on paper

In my drawer

They sing to my soul

Whilst fingers longing to play

Frozen Pushed in my pockets

Trying to thaw

Staring to still ice Oceans

And walking aimlessly through dunes

 A curious observer of

beauty and tunes

Within this shame

Should I hide or cover?

Or listen through candlelight

In granite walls

Guitar strumming souls

Willing me to recover

I Frightened so many away

When I was

Irrecoverably broken

And even now

In this bay'

Where you kept me

In Silent retort

I still cannot defend myself

I was not at your court

I continue to walk

In my own space

Of too many thoughts

Whilst fingers of fiddlers

Offer me their heart

And sharp diamond skies pull

The waves to stillness

And in this ever present

I realise

Peace and silence

were never apart

Background; As I started to recover through winter, I was introduced to Spotify and started listening to music again acoustic folk guitar I would write down new artists I heard and put them in the drawer; it was the start of discovering enjoyment again; it fed my soul; along with long walks. My head felt numb and icy but I could feel some sharp happiness in the distance like I was watching it from behind a rock. I knew I had to keep going including battling all the shame and stigma that constantly arose from feeling judged and abandoned whilst my brain began to find its way home.

Chapter 9

Guide To Nutrition

Section 1: The Gut/ Brain and Mental Health Diets

N.B read section 2of this chapter if you are highly anxious and this section when you are in recovery or get your carers/ family to read on your behalf.

I'm not sure why nutrition has been left until Chapter 9 as it is **so important** for mental health. In fact, along with the **Safety, Nurture, Connection, Structure (SNCS)** my process to recovery included

1. Making sure I felt safe by having people willing to support me .
2. Sort out medication/ alternative treatments if necessary.
3. Nutrition.
4. The therapy I was having was starting to take effect.
5. Regular structure of activities, meditation and breathing.
6. Happiness and an ability to manage/accept emotional health.

Nutrition will also include alternative herbs or plant- based supplements which can offer relief and healing for anxiety and depression. Some of the suggestions therefore overlap with the end of chapter four (alternative medication.)

When you are highly anxious, your body is working hard, over alert and constantly in a state of fight or flight. It is a chemical reaction within the brain between the frontal cortex and the amygdala/ hippocampus communication process; also mentioned in chapter one. It is usually triggered by an emotional event, hormonal shift, long term stress or poor thought habits.

The brain is being told there is a threat. For many of us to be told to 'snap out of it' is impossible because it feels like such a permanent state that built chemically within our bodies, often unaware to us, over months or years.

When someone says **"Just get on with it,"** of course that is all we want to do, but this says more about the person and their ignorance than it does about you. Firstly, they are scared and, secondly, they haven't put themselves in your shoes. Either way it is just a totally useless sentiment and should be ignored completely.

Cortisol is our stress hormone produced by the adrenal gland and it increases blood sugar to prepare us literally to 'fight or flight' a life-threatening situation.

Often in our modern lifestyles however, it is not a life-threatening situation; it is a busy life and a busy mind that has caused this and is telling the body there is danger. **The brain is like a child, it believes what it is told and acts upon the signal.**

Eventually, in this 'fight or flight' state **Cortisol (*)** starts to run low and this can create a body that is not fully functioning and is exhausted causing **adrenal fatigue**. At this point the body shows signs of inflammation which is the precursor to many physical and mental diseases.

(*)https://www.merriamwebster.com/dictionary/cortisolCortisol definition is - a glucocorticoid $C_{21}H_{30}O_5$ produced by the adrenal cortex upon stimulation by ACTH that mediates various metabolic processes (such as gluconeogenesis), has anti-inflammatory and immunosuppressive properties, and whose levels in the blood may become elevated in response to physical or psychological stress — called also hydrocortisone.

Studies on anxiety often point to low levels of cortisol in the body. This may also be associated with a malfunctioning endocrine system and hormonal imbalances.
(https://www.psychologytoday.com/us/blog/the-athletes-way/201707/cortisol-harvard-study-finds-moderate-response-)

As well as stress many studies point to other essential nutrients that are lacking in the body. For example, low levels of omega 3, B vitamins essential for the endocrine system, amongst others, have been linked to poor mental

health...(https://www.psychologytoday.com/us/blog/the-athletes-way/201707/cortisol-harvard-study-finds-moderate-response-)
Understanding nutrition, depression and mental illnesses (nih.gov)

Looking at the food or supplements we eat can have a major impact on mental disharmony, restoring some of these imbalances and calming the body. Taking regular time out to calm the body through meditation, for example, also go hand in hand with good nutrition.

Depression has some opposing symptoms when compared to anxiety but **both are associated with an imbalance and/or inflammation in the brain.** These symptoms include no energy or enthusiasm for anything, as well as feeling sad and scared you will also be physically exhausted.

Both conditions bring poor eating habits and can cause weight loss or gain. It's **hard to follow any healthy eating plan as most of the time you just don't care if you're overeating or spending many days without good nutrition.**

The key to some people's mental health issues may lie in their gut. Poor diets have been linked with moderate to severe anxiety and depression all the way to Schizophrenia. Gut Bacteria And Schizophrenia (https;//theceliacmd.com).

Exploring these possibilities has to be a must for you or your carer to get on the road to recovery. Years of stress and poor eating habits can lead to '**Leaky Gut Syndrome**' or 'intestinal hyper permeability'. It is thought that this condition can cause leakage of waste into the rest of the body through the intestinal wall linings. This can cause a host of problems including anxiety and depression. These ideas are relatively new and research really kicked off in the last decade on the subject. The news is positive though.

Giulia Enders in her book 'GUT' explains that there is a communicating channel via a major nerve channel known as The

'**Vagus Nerve**' which links the gut to the brain. The gut links with some part of the brain and it comes of **no surprise that these include the frontal cortex, the amygdala and the hippocampus.**

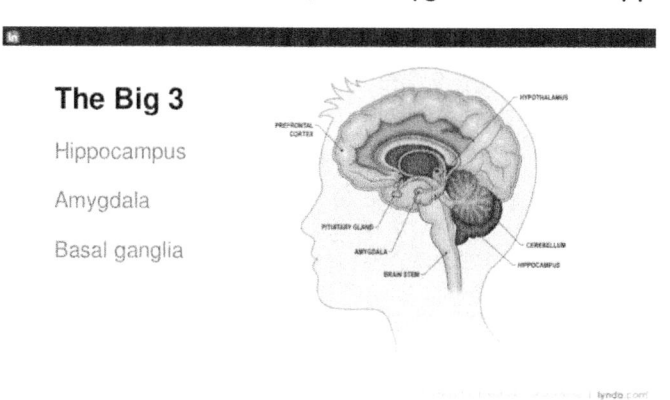

The Big 3

Hippocampus

Amygdala

Basal ganglia

Enders goes onto explain that **the brain is one of the most insulated organs in the body,** it needs good communication channels from the rest of the body to know how everything is doing, and because the gut has a vast surface containing many nerves it can collect a lot of information for the brain.

It will communicate **only the important parts** via the Vagus nerve and finally Thalamus gland. The information is used by the brain to form our response to the outside world. **So, say that again?**

'**The information is used by the brain to produce a response to the outside world.**' In other words, bad gut health equals bad brain response to the world.

Fascinatingly, the brain will call back on the gut to reserve some energy to deal with this stress so the gut slows digestion and reduces blood flow and mucous. So can you see how physiology and emotions interact in this process.

The gut's expectation to limit its activities and reserve energy because of stress is a **short-term response** bu,t if **emotional** distress continues, long term then **the brain will continue to ask the gut to respond.** The gut can respond in many different ways to stress like getting rid of food quickly to save energy (diarrhoea) or slowing down (constipation). It also changes the microbial activity (bacteria in the gut that breaks down our food), and creates imbalances where bad microbes can thrive and good ones are in short supply.

Over time, if these short- term processes remain long term, physical damage can occur in the way of a weaker protective layer and limited blood supply. **So now this damage is communicated back to the brain affecting the way we respond to the world.**

The damage and thinning of the gut is often referred **to as Leaky Gut Syndrome.** It means the gut is not working and toxins can leak into the blood stream causing many chronic health conditions

So simply; **The Gut feels bad, it communicates this to the brain, the brain signals to us that we feel bad; and then we feel bad.**

Enders believes from her research that not a great deal is known as to why anti-depressants work except for the changes they have to our feel good chemicals '**serotonin.**' Some research has shown that it makes the nerve passages more 'neuro plastic' (flexible) so easing some of the long-term patterns that the nerve carries.

Enders comments on **the physical side effects of anti-depressants which often go to the gut and produce side effects such as bloating, weight gain and diarrhoea.**

'The gut brain' has become a new term after the discovery of more neuro receptors than the brain itself. So interestingly we have two brains that link producing serotonin.

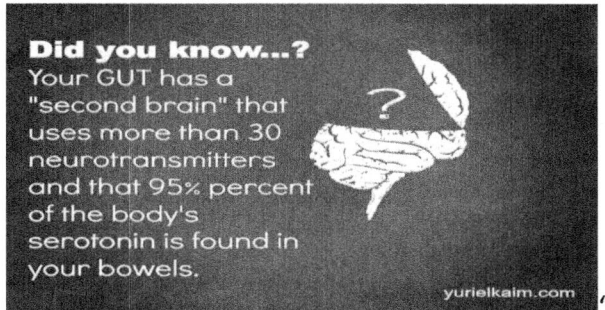

Did you know...? Your GUT has a "second brain" that uses more than 30 neurotransmitters and that 95% percent of the body's serotonin is found in your bowels.

"95% of the serotonin we manufacture is in our gut." Enders 'Gut' page 130)

Essentially, the gut produces *serotonin which is a signalling molecule,* if the signals are good to the brain in turn, or in theory, the brain will respond well. This idea is being looked at for mild anxiety and depression to more severe cases, **which is how my journey into poor mental health started by taking an antibiotic that wiped out all my good and bad bacteria of which I probably had a limited supply as a postpartum new Mother.**

All new Doctors should be aware that new Mothers may be more sensitive to side effects of medication because their supplies of goodness are being prioritised for their offspring. Unless it is absolutely essential, avoid these harsh pharmaceuticals like antibiotics and steroids in this vulnerable state.

As well as Enders we also have the research and practice of Doctor Michael Moseley's 'The Clever Guts Diet' which offers a process to repair the lining of your gut through good nutrition and in return produce good mental health.

It involves a different diet and no sugar or alcohol but for a relatively short time; 6 weeks. I only became aware of this when I was recovering and I did the clever guts diet, but bearing in mind I was well and even though I was still on medication I felt real clarity in my head and happiness. I had a lot more energy and went to the toilet regularly and easily. I am due to do it again soon and would recommend it to anyone.

What I want to say is that Moseley's gut repair diet actually doesn't make you feel hungry; despite the 'no processed sugar' and I believe this is because there are lots of healthy fats in it, which I will explain later.

The secondary part of this process is recreating our gut with the range of 'microbes' in our gut that are needed. Microbes are simply bacteria and we need a good range of good and bad bacteria to function. Fascinatingly as Deepak Chopra states **95% of our body's response is microbial**.

The gut diet reinstates these microbes which help us feel full of energy and by additionally working on negative thought patterns. The possibility is that you can and will work your way to happiness possibly through growing a new gut lining.

As well as Moseley, I also love the recipes and philosophies in "The Microbiome Solution." Chutkan, who wrote this book, was actually a clinical gut Doctor who chose a different approach when she saw some of her patients with severe Colitis and Irritable Bowel Syndrome (IBS), getting better whilst using alternative treatments. At first, she had literally covered her face in shock fearing the consequences of such an irresponsible action.

The pharmaceuticals she prescribed were anti -inflammatory amongst others to keep the patient ticking over like all pharmaceuticals seem to do but like many pharmaceuticals **there is no intention to heal**.

On that note it may come of no surprise to learn that the big pharmaceutical companies have no philanthropic objectives to get you well. Originally maybe, but now with billion dollar industries and commission led surgery practices, your health has been lost in their pursuit for profit.

'The 100 year Lie' by Randall Fitzgerald is a real eye opener to read, it confirms what many are starting to come to believe that

the food and medical industries manipulate our lives presenting themselves as beneficial when in fact they have done much harm to our health.

If you are healthy perhaps you don't need to look at this but if you are suffering with mental and physical health issues this subject is worth exploring.

Masanobu Fukuoka in his amazing book about natural farming **'Sowing Seeds in The Desert,'** describes the modern medical system as a giant octopus congratulating itself whilst chewing off its own legs. I love that and what an inspiring book this is. He expresses his concerns that whilst medicine has reached such advancements people are actually getting sicker from the increased use of medicines and chemicals in our food. It appears that getting back to eating less chemicals and natural foods also seems to be an opening to good mental health.

In Chutkan's book she links anxiety and depression to gut balance and believes that because the gut is the major producer of serotonin then treating gut health may be a more effective treatment than simply prescribing anti-depressants.

Chutkan's advice and recipes are great and involve **lots of good fats** and no or low sugar (like Moseley). She also offers the correct advice on probiotic supplements. Fascinatingly we need at least 50 billion probiotics of the right variety to help long term gut dysbiosis. **In other words, some supplements just won't do anything or are irrelevant to treating certain gut conditions.**

When the body is out of balance our hormonal system will be out, so let's talk about hormones particularly this troublesome little one...the thyroid.

This little gland in our neck affects significantly more women than men but most research points to the fact that many people may have an undiagnosed thyroid condition and guess what; *an imbalance of the thyroid is connected to poor mental health both depression and anxiety...*

Let's look at Kinsey Jackson's book 'The Thyroid Reboot,' many books are starting to be written around this subject because we have an epidemic of thyroid disease in the Western world which seems to have coincided with an increase in depression related illnesses...**why**?

According to Jackson, thyroid issues can be misdiagnosed as a depression, anxiety, bi-polar amongst others. Why am I telling you this? I have a non -toxic goitre or a lump on my Thyroid, so I have always been interested in how the thyroid would interlink with other health issues as the goitre came up during a particularly stressful time in my life when I was 'burning the candle at both ends,' In my late 20s.

What I found fascinating is that literature that I have studied about the gut / brain link and the thyroid all seem to offer a very similar approach to renewing this area of our body that can affect so much of our mental and physical health and it is this; <u>**healthy fats, low sugar and lots of fresh vegetables.**</u> This can not only provide a cure to 'leaky gut' but also can make your body and mind thrive. BOOM! here we have a potential brain restorer.

So, in a nutshell, these are the interesting points Jackson makes in her book about The Thyroid:

The thyroid is a butterfly shaped gland in base of the neck is part of our endocrine system; a system that tells our body what to do; it controls body temperature and metabolism amongst other functions.

The major two hormones it produces are T3 and T4 which help deliver **O2 and energy** to every cell. The liver for example turns T4 to T3; **so bad liver function could limit this process.** This little gland absorbs iodine from our food for use combined with amino acids to make the T4 and T3.

It is complex but T3 is the active hormone and T4, which is produced in greater amounts, can transport round the body as a backup waiting to be turned into T3 if needed. **Poor lifestyle, including bad liver function, inflammation, poor nutrition slows down this process.**

Above the thyroid in the top of the head are two other glands; pituitary and hypothalamus (see illustration at the beginning of this chapter) they both orchestrate this process and release 'Thyroid Releasing Hormone' to start this process. Most thyroid function blood tests just test the TSH not the T3 or T4 levels (which would indicate the thyroids inability to produce both these important hormones) *hence misdiagnosing potential thyroid disease is common because blood tests are simply not that thorough.*

Mood and sleep are just 2 of the outcomes that can occur from these imbalances and guess what? **They get diagnosed as depression/ anxiety.**

You can ask for your T3 and T4 levels to be checked if needed but you may have to pay for these additional tests.

Auto immune disease in the thyroid occurs when the immune system gets confused and starts attacking the thyroid gland itself. **Hypothyroid (under active)** - think depressed low mood, lethargic and **hyperthyroid (over active)** - think anxious, agitated, insomnia skinny. Both conditions according to Jackson cannot be cured **but they can be put into remission.**

Jackson herself had hypothyroidism for years. She lost a lot of her hair was moody, had arthritis, lupus (auto immune) and brain fog.

Jackson's initial hair loss was treated by injecting steroids into her head, leaving scars and doing nothing. She eventually got diagnosed by a good naturopath and changed her diet completely.

If you think your gut needs repair avoid **gluten and some grains.** Interestingly in Jackson's explains that gluten contains a protein called **gliadin** which stimulates another gut protein in the gut known as Zonulin. This opens up the gut out too often and can damage the intestinal wall allowing bacteria to get through to the blood; the immune system then responds by producing **inflammation.**

Gliadin also looks like thyroid tissue which means our immune system starts to attack the gliadin in the blood as it believes the thyroid is trying to take over.

Now sadly according to Jackson 50% of people who have issues with gluten will also have issues with **dairy**. The **casein** protein in dairy also looks similar to your thyroid on a cellular level so the immune system again will attack it as a threat of overproduction. Lactose can also affect the gut balance as well.

Viruses such as EBV; Epstein Bar Virus, a nasty little virus from the herpes family that can be undiagnosed for years, can attack and start the downfall of the intestine wall. There are herbs and life style changes that can kill these viruses but for many people they do not notice these viruses are lurking until severe symptoms kick in.

Here's something also really interesting in Jackson's book; Iodine is from the same family as Chlorine, Bromine and Fluorine the halogen gp on the periodic table. **The thyroid cannot distinguish the difference and will absorb chlorine and fluoride as it does iodine which ultimately attack the gland**; *so change your toothpaste, filter your water, change to plant based cleaning products even if you don't think your thyroid is out. These chemicals may be encouraging the imbalance in your body.*

Last but not least, **sugar,** which we all know is pretty bad. I recently read **Paul Mckenna's 'Get Control of Sugar Now!'** I honestly would recommend this book, it's great. McKenna really puts it in your face that Sugar really is a drug and when you get to the other side of the addiction and taste it again it tastes quite alien.

If you want to improve your mental health through diet; processed sugar has to go. All is not lost though as some dark chocolate is not only acceptable but has calming and beneficial effects on anxiety.

<u>Depression and Dark Chocolate | Psychology Today</u> (Gary Drevitch Jan 2020)

Try organic cocoa, honey cinnamon and hot oak milk, for example..

Jackson, Chutkan and Moseley provide some sweet but nutritious snacks that are not high in sugar but satisfy that sweet tooth.

Again, all good advice whether your mental health is directly linked to your thyroid or not.

I just want to give you a quote from Jackson's book in regards to healthy fats and low sugar. It is the same sentiment as Michael Moseley, Chutkan, Enders and Asprey. Put more good fats into your diet take OUT sugar and bad fats/ processed foods and you won't put on weight (unless you need to) you will lose weight and feel more in balance hormonally and have greater brain function;

'Although touted as unhealthy for decades, saturated fats are used for hormonal and energy production, cell membrane formation and many more biological functions in the body. In short saturated fats are far from unhealthy, they are actually some of the healthiest fats we can consume for optimizing our thyroid and overall health.' (*)

*(please note Omega 3 is a polyunsaturated fat but is still one of the only healthy ones)

Now I know that was a bit of a lecture above or to some it may seem because perhaps you cannot achieve miracles straight away in this area. **When you feel severely agitated and sleepless or just like a tonne of bricks with no energy or motivation it is hard to put any plan in place.**

I remember eating oatcakes, nuts, fruit and raw carrots out of pure necessity. I would only cook (badly) if my son was around. When you are depressed, you may gorge food.

I personally suffered weight loss but used to force certain foods down me as I thought I would probably die if I didn't; and that was my health anxiety kicking in.

Sometimes you may eat a lot, some days little and that's ok… tricking your metabolism by keeping it away from patterns and changing isn't always a bad thing. **'Fast This Way' by Dave Asprey** discusses this in his book about improving our health and mental clarity.

Whilst it has been proven that fasting can sometimes help our bodies; when you are suffering daily with awful mental afflictions, your diet will almost be poor. So, explore some of the ideas I am offering here or get anyone that is looking after you to do this as changing one or two habits can lead to a calmer or more energised you.

For example, sweet potatoes are anti-inflammatory. I had a client at work with severe arthritis. She swapped white potato portions for sweet potatoes and her arthritis became less inflamed after two weeks.

What I want to do for carers and suffers is give some basic essentials that can help improve gut health and mental health. If you can't eat everyday just try some basics; snacks; **nuts, seeds, oats even avocados will push great amounts of nutrition in your body in small amounts.**

I also want to mention foraging as well as certain and simple hedgerow plants are highly nutritious and foraging is part of my daily ritual now; a basic knowledge of a few leaves per day may help to restore some balance.

Further reading and an easy picture reference will be added about foraging as well as other relevant books at the end of this book. You may wish to explore when you are in a better frame of mind.

Basic plants like Dandelion, Nettle, Cleavers (sticky goose grass) and finally GRASS -yes GRASS - (see K. Blair) are easy plants to collect but have massive nutritional and anti-inflammatory properties.

'The 100 Year Lie', by Randall Fitzgerald, mentioned previously, despite being written decades ago will also clarify the gut work this book makes you understand. Fitzgerald endorses that processed and over chemicalised food and medication in our system makes the body act in strange ways. Some of these chemicals imitate hormone responses and so lose our bodies natural responses throwing our whole system out of balance.

Chronic Fatigue At the end of section 2 I will be recommending some plant- based remedies and I want to mention phytonutrients compounds found in plants and glyconutrients which are plant sugars linked in chains. Rather than boosting our immune systems like some plants; Echinacea for example which can actually create an overreaction or inflammatory response if given to an already inflamed system *(The Lost Book Of Herbal Remedies page 72),* glyconutrients help encourage cell communication this is great for Fibromyalgia, hormonal imbalances and many auto immune issues.

Glyconutrients work by stimulating the immune system then encourage the colon to increase its microbial activity. They can take a few weeks to a few months to work so be patient. Why do I mention this?

A lot of people who become **physically ill then become depressed.** This stands to reason after what we have just explored in this chapter .So the best way out is **to treat the physical condition** and the depression will be alleviated. My recommendation wholeheartedly for chronic fatigue, Fibromyalgia, ME and other auto immune issues is **Ambrotose by a company called Mannatech.**

Mannatech believe that some of our modern foods do not carry all the phytonutrients needed for cell communication and so a glyconutrient encourages this process within the body. Yes, I am going to stick my neck out here and recommend a product. It is quite expensive and would cost around 100 GBP a month but you may only have to take it for three months. The proof is in the pudding.

I used it once for chronic fatigue in my early 30s following a bout of severe glandular fever in my 20s. I then suffered Post Viral Fatigue about ten years after.

I was a wreck, I slept at 5pm every day, some days were worse than others. I was managing to get myself to work but I felt like a piece of lead. Blood tests came back normal but I didn't. I was recommended this and after taking a small amount daily for two weeks my energy started to change. I didn't use this for my severe anxiety as it seemed to make me more restless but if I have any bouts of fatigue now then I will definitely turn to it.

If **Ambrotose** is out of your budget then look at **Reishi Mushroom** (quality supplements and tinctures from a reputable source) also know as 'the mushroom of immortality' it is an *adaptogenic which helps stress, inflammation, increased cortisol levels and fatigue, adrenal fatigue and immune support. And helps a whole host of conditions including cancer but this amazing mushroom improves depression, anxiety and insomnia.*

'Many scientists will say there is no evidence of Glyconutrients working but go online and you will find a whole community that use Ambrotose and Reishi for a wide range of conditions from fibromyalgia, hypo/hyperthyroidism, Multiple Sclerosis to Cancer. Give it a go and don't underestimate the power of the medicinal mushrooms. (also see Fantastic Fungi on Netflix.)

In her amazing reference book 'The Lost Book OF Herbal Remedies' Nicole Apelian (listed at the end) uses Reishi Mushroom double extracted tinctures for her Multiple Sclerosis. She uses it along with **Lion's Mane which has similar benefits to Reishi.** I will list these at the end. Also see 'Fantastic Fungi on Netflix.

Chapter 9 Continued...

Section2; Simple steps to follow right now.

After explaining about the gut link with the brain I'm keeping this section simple as I know how difficult it is to keep up basic care when you are anxious or depressed.

I will give you the 'whys' and summarise at the end the foods to buy if you can manage this. I am doing this with an intention of trying to calm those adrenals down which produce our stress responses in our bodies. This along with correct breathing all contribute to feeding the brain the right messages that everything is ok.

So here are some simple rules that may change your body to a calmer less inflamed anxious system.

- Let's start with **drink 8 glasses of filtered water a day**; basic hydration is the key to a properly functioning body.

- **The B's** (the B12s and the magnesium rich food) can possibly turn the tables for you. For example, the B12 deficiency may be a prime cause of your mental health issues. Try to load up with a range of B vitamins in your diet. **Vitamin B is water soluble like Vitamin C so you can't overdose. Seeds and nuts** contain a lot of vitamin Bs. Vitamin B is found in a lot of protein (including oily fish) and dairy products, marmite and, for vegetarians, eggs, nuts, seeds and Veggie mite drinks every day, Vitamin B supplements can be useful to support mental health; particularly **B12**. There are some important links and we need to look at all aspects of diet that may improve the debilitation of poor mental health. Some of the evidence is staggering so whilst trying keep good nutrition practices when in this state adding a B12 supplement may be a good path to follow. https://www.b12deficiency.info/b12-and-mental-health

- **The Cs to boost the immune system. Take small amounts of vitamin C Powder every other day or when you feel ill.** Yes, not tablets – **powder** - it will pump vitamin C into your body faster than any tablet. Suzanne Humphries' study on whooping cough shows this to be the best way to take this vitamin to improve chronic health conditions. Vitamin C powder is relatively cheap. A lot of mental health issues are accompanied by pure immune response; whether it is the chicken first or the egg is not always clear but we just need to treat and get you on the road to recovery.

- **The Omega 3's;** eating **oily fish twice a week** (sardines on toast easy and cheap) takes down our inflammatory conditions and reduces anxiety and depression; Remember depression has been linked to inflammation in the brain. If you don't eat fish or meat, **Omega 3s are found in most nuts, particularly walnuts, chia seeds and linseeds they are**

all great source of nutrition and highly beneficial for your heart. These "good" fats help improve cholesterol levels, lower blood pressure and reduce inflammation; thus, reducing your overall risk of heart disease. Since omega-3 fatty acids have such beneficial effects in lowering inflammation, getting your daily dose of omega-3s can help reduce effects of arthritis, reducing pain and tenderness. Having inadequate omega-3s in your diet may increase your risk of depression, since these fats are essential for normal neurological function by helping nerve cells communicate.
'https://www.livestrong.com/article/492098-omega-3-fatty-acids-peanuts/

- **Magnesium** or lack of Mg is massively linked with depression as well as ADHD and many hormonal imbalances. It is worth exploring. It can be found in **seeds of course and leafy veg**. Low levels of magnesium in our soils means the required amounts are not transferring to the plants that we eat. **Try and eat organic, grow your own and forage** to get higher quantities of magnesium. Soak in the bath with affordable magnesium salts. Magnesium is often referred to as nature's tranquiliser. Magnesium works particularly well to help you unwind when it is supplied in a high strength powder form of bisglycinate and combined with B vitamins, vitamin C, taurine and theanine - a calming amino acid found naturally in tea. Most Western diets are low in magnesium.

- **Coconut Oil** is full of nutrients and is a great hormone balancer also when heated (unlike Olive Oil) it does not lose its nutrients and is linked to brain health, helps heart and yeast infections such as Candida. Coconut oil is a gut repairer and is used extensively in any gut repair diet.

- **Turmeric;** Curcumin in turmeric is a powerful antioxidant, anti-inflammatory and limits the growth of bad bacteria pathogens and fungi and protects the intestinal wall, so going back to the gut link with mental health this is a very useful supplement to take. Don't want to cook with it? Buy capsules from ebay fairly cheap but always with black pepper in otherwise turmeric doesn't activate; the other oil that activates turmeric is coconut oil; so, if you are feeling up to it cook a veg dahl with coconut oil and turmeric; highly nutritious and calming.

- **Kombucha;** I cannot tell you enough about the amazing benefits of this easy to prepare and cheap 'culture.' It has been linked with the improvement and even cures of many diseases of the physical and mental body, it was used before the war and originally came in from The East. However, when sugar shortages came in during the war it phased out but is now making a comeback along with fermented foods in general. See the book for some really basic guides to producing it. It is easy to prepare and really helped me to focus on good health whilst preparing my teas and watching the Kombucha grow. Most people find it a bit slimy but I have learned to love the prep of mine. Also here is the fabulous magic; when you prepare a batch it reproduces so you end up with many cultures and you can either make more or give it away to friends. No wonder the big pharmas want to keep you away from this miraculous little culture it is virtually free and creates abundance in front of your eyes.

- **Keffir;** similar to Kombucha but grown in milk rather than sugary black tea. Again, amazing effects on your gut biome and in turn physical and mental health.

- **Sauerkraut** Another Eastern dietary delight and so easy to make. Chop an organic cabbage, carrots, beetroot or any veg up, in thick or thin pieces and rub it with around two tablespoons of salt. Load it into a big glass jar pushing it firmly down and leaving a 3cm gap at the top and seal the jar. Release the lid and turn a couple of times over two weeks. The fermentation sours the cabbage in a week or two and it is so good for the gut. **Add grated ginger and turmeric root for a healthy zing.**

- Foraging; (*) see 'Plants And Us' at the end)
  When I was recovering, my neighbour Raymond, who is 83, and a keen forager asked me if I would like to learn about edible wild plants. So started a great friendship. He has taught me so much over the last four years and introduced me to many of the books I have referenced in this chapter. He is truly lovely company and reads way more than me. It is so good listening to his vast knowledge and I have filmed some of our lessons together.

  Foraging has become part of my life. My son and I often pick wild plants and eat or cook them. Of course, you need to take precautions so at the end of this section I have recommended 4 basic plants that will blow the socks off any plant -based products from the Supermarket.

  Foraged plants are so fully enriched with minerals and vitamins and they are free. As well as this Foraging gets you out in nature which is where our souls long to be. Dandelion in salad; a nettle soup weekly, Cleavers in the spring and summer (known as sticky goose grass) in cooking or smoothies and **Grass** ; yes Grass, one of the most nutritious plants (*see Katrina Blair; The Wild Wisdom Of Weeds*) can all be juiced with apple too. One of the best books (In my opinion), for learning about edible plants in this country is 'Hedgerow Medicine' by Julie and Matthew Seal. Seal has produced an easy to understand highly fascinating book that sticks to the basics but will surprise you with just how much these wild plants can heal us. It has a great description of **Nettles, Dandelion** and **Cleavers**.

It is estimated that there are about 350,000 species of existing plants (including seed plants, bryophytes, and ferns), among which 287,655 species have been identified as of 2004 [1] provide amazing tonics for the body. https://www.ncbi.nlm.nih.gov/pmc/articles/PMC4020364/

- **Fat yes Fat;** If you are anxious don't worry too much about the fat contents your body will be working hard and over running its adrenals so you will need good fats. Fats are found in seeds and nuts. **Good fats will calm and nourish your system and keep you away from sugar cravings**. Saying that I don't mean drink cups of it but what you will notice in all the gut repair programmes (see section 1) and hormone balance diets include a good amount of healthy fats such as **coconut oil, olive oil, walnut oil, pumpkin oil and avocado oils**. They will fill you up and give you the energy you need to get through the next day. Surprisingly good oils help detox the system as well which will help the gut lining. Walnut oil for example is useful for eliminating parasites.

- **Cocoa;** Wow, just wow! This is a great winner for mental health. Cocoa is proving to be an amazing micro biome builder; it contains a high content of minerals and the more research being done the more they are finding out that this little plant is way more than a superfood. Sprinkle it on your yoghurt; make a drink with honey and cinnamon to calm the nerves. **This is the key with Cocoa is the calm.** Buy organic; sadly, normal Cocoa does not have the same nutrition. Go to for reasonable priced organic Cocoa and seeds go to; https://wwwbuywholefoodsonline.co.uk

https://www.nutritionadvance.com/cocoa-powder-nutrition/

- *Drinks*; Honey in tea instead of sugar; add oat milk if you are chesty then don't overload the dairy. Cups of tea are comfort if you are a carer just sit next to them quietly. If they don't like tea give them Chicory which is another substance that is full of minerals and will repair the gut, as well as Camomile to calm or fruit teas. Green tea is a great detox but has caffeine in so be careful.

- If anxious coffee may overload the adrenals too much; stick to simple drinks; comfort them it is not life threatening if they know someone is next to them and prepared to wait...
- **Fruit veg, veg and veg.** If you can't be bothered to cook eat raw carrots, raw any veg (except potato). Preferably washed and organic.
- **Nuts and Seed;** Again, if you can't be bothered to cook have nuts and seeds in your cupboard

Alternative medicine herbs to try for anxiety and depression

When trying any of the following of course check with a professional and check that it is ok to take with your current meds e.g., St John's Wort cannot be taken with anti-depressants and CBD cannot be taken alongside Benzodiazepines. Don't expect instant results for example Holy Basil tea can calm cortisol levels straight away as well as numerous other benefits but for general anxiety disorder it can take up to 60 days of up to 1800mg dose to see the effects; so be patient and try one at a time but don't forget just because **we have lost some of the benefits of these alternatives it does not mean they are not powerful.**

Some may not suit you they may give you side effects but the difference is there are generally less side effects and their objective will be to heal whereas pharmaceuticals generally aren't to balance restore and heal but to stop or mask the undesired effects. With anxiety and depression, of course, this is a great relief but long term natural solutions may be a better option.

- **CBD Oil**; I mentioned this in the medication section; when coming off my meds slowly I introduced CBD capsules. Some of the research on this has shown spectacular results in not only calming but curing anxiety and depression, as well as other debilitating health conditions.
  As I said at the summary at the end of this chapter The Holland and Barratt capsules have helped me but some people think that the quality is paramount but it can be expensive. I would recommend reducing pharmaceutical medication as sometimes the side effects from these meds won't disappear with the use of CBD so you will not appreciate the benefit. Go to the help groups on social media for help and support.
  Remember many people have found this an immense relief from years of anxiety and physical pain. The person in this article found a change within a week
  https://inews.co.uk/inews-lifestyle/people/ive-virtually-cured-my-20-year-battle-with-anxiety-and-back-pain-)
  after being on anti-depressants for 20 years.

- **Holy Basil (Ocimum Tenuiflorum (Tulsi)**; someone introduced this to me late in my recovery but still prone to rare but severe bouts of anxiety and having to use pharmaceuticals, I found this a god send. I was totally shocked I had never heard of it before. It is ayurvedic herb from India. In India it is revered and is said in the Hindu community as the 'Incomparable one' the one that 'Cures all;' It has a strong clove like aroma. It's all over uses for physical, chemical and psychological conditions makes it very powerful.

For anxiety and depression, it has been compared to the effects of Diazepam but without the withdrawals. Clinical research shows it does not have any interactions with other drugs but although considered safe effects on pregnant women and children are unknown.

A cup of tea made with 2 to 3 teaspoons will naturally lower cortisol levels and have a strong effect on promoting sleep and calming. For general anxiety disorders a dose of between 600mg to 1800mg tablets is recommended per day and the effects can take up to 60 days (similar to anti-depressants). As well as this this herb is rich in vitamin A and C, calcium, Zinc and Chlorophyll. It boosts the immune system and it is anti-bacterial, anti-viral, anti-inflammatory, it lowers cholesterol and the effects of diabetes. It is being researched for cancer and helps the body protect itself from the effects of heavy metals and pollutions. It brightens the mind; the list is endless

- **Ashwagandha**; Buy this amazing herb in powder form (cheapest way) I recently had a bout of anxiety (yep still get it sometimes) and I treated it with Ashwagandha and CBD capsules. It took a few days to kick in and I was of course working on my inner child state and understanding the triggers.
Ashgwanda has many benefits including studies linked to improved thyroid balance but *be careful as this is only studies with Hypothyroidism.*

If you have hyperthyroidism, it may make it worse. So, if you are unsure talk to a professional on the subject; a qualified herbalist can guide you and monitor you.
It is worth looking into micro dosing as the benefits are amazing. Don't take if you are pregnant.
Ashwagandha has a cortisol (stress hormone) lowering effect on the body; It is also a blood sugar balancer. These two effects are great for stress and anxiety I put a teaspoonseach morning (when my anxiety was highest) of it in an oat smoothie with banana as it's quite bitter. I also added **Wheatgrass and Moringa** other high nutritional plants you may want to explore. If Ashwagandha does not work for you also see Holy Basil as this will lower cortisol levels. Healthline.com/nutrition/12-proven-ashwagandha-benefits#4 and to buy the powder go to buyWholefoodsonline.co.uk.

- St John's Wort (Hypericum perforatum)
  This natural remedy can be very effective (if you are not on medication already). This is really worth a try and can also be effective for menopause as well as insomnia and has been used for hundreds of years it is thought that hypericum and hyperforin in the plant act as messengers to the nervous system increasing mood.
  This may well be worth a shot before considering pharmaceutical medication; although in some countries St John's Wort is prescribed through the Doctors. Although it has few side effects it MUST NOT be taken with anti-depressants so please check all the information before taking.
  (Do not take two weeks prior to surgery, on HIV medication,or if you are on anti-depressants already. Not to be used with bipolar disorder).

- **Nutri Adrenal;** A glandular therapy uses animal tissue concentrates to support the function of the corresponding human gland. Bovine glands are used as they are very similar to human glands

  In studies, glandulars have been shown to be stable in the gut, survive the conditions of the gut, and an amount of the extract will pass intact into the bloodstream. However, this involves an animal product. I myself found taking this with high Vitamin B had a calming effect on anxiety.

  For vegetarians and vegans, I researched the internet and found a really revered formula which actually has Ashgwanda, Rhodiola Rosea, Gotu Kola and Schizsandara. This supplement is called 'Adrenal Support' by 1 Body. There are many reviews saying that people experiencing anxiety and various thyroid issues had found this a miracle calmer it could be a good alternative as a vegetarian adrenal support. What I most liked about this supplement and/or Nutri Adrenal is they seem to have a calming effect on people with stress and anxiety and an energising effect on people with chronic fatigue and depression.

- https://www.amazon.co.uk/Adrenal-Support-Vegetarian-containing-Astragalus/dp/B0131EDZKS/ref=sr_1_1_sspa?crid=1AVR48994B0BZ&dc

Avoid;

- Food, drink and drugs can also be used to mask our emotional pains. When we get into feeding our nurturing vacuums (see chapter 7) we need quick addictive fixes that will ease the craving momentarily. There is no judgement here but, if you are in mental distress, they will be aggravating your condition greatly.

- *If you regularly feed yourself alcohol / cigarettes* you are probably not allowing your body to process emotional pain. *Numbing and filling your vacuums with a quick fix causes agitation and ill health.* **Once it empties you find yourself in more pain; a bit like the side effects of some medications.** The result may be an uncontrollable flow of pain. Alcohol puts strain on the liver and increasing likelihood of digestive cancers; larynx, stomach, bowl but also upsets our natural biome and ultimately affects our immune system.

Alcohol more importantly can affect our brains, over use can produce long term brain damage. **Forgive yourself for occasional blow outs** but don't use it as a support because it does the exact opposite; alcohol is a depressant. If you are using alcohol excessively regularly come off it slowly; don't just stop. This is no lecture. I could not touch alcohol when I was ill but, throughout my life, I have binged on it and used it as an emotional anaesthetic so I know the pain it brings.

- Cigarettes contain 4000 toxic chemicals and are one of the most poisonous substances that we ingest on the planet. When smoking you're poisoning your system.
  Nicotine is one of the most addictive substances, it appears to calm you for a short-lived period but then takes you into more of an anxious state than your normal levels of anxiety... It tricks your brain receptors into releasing a bit of serotonin before it hurls you into an anxious withdrawal. In other words, you are poisoning and agitating an already suffering system. As an ex-smoker again I'm certainly not lecturing you but as part of reducing anxiety it's important that you get help to let go of this destructive habit to find peace in your body. I do get that this may seem your only vice at the moment, but it is a trick. It has tricked you into thinking it is a comfort when in fact it is your enemy. No judgement though if you can only cut down right now, do

just that and eat as much good mood enhancing food as possible.

- If you are looking after someone who is mentally suffering make them **soup**; things that are easy to eat with lots of nutrition, **vegetable dahl, oat cakes**; they may not want to eat but just give them that simple, easily absorbable nutrition.

- Finally, for those who are suffering and read these ideas for nutrition and health try and engage in something like researching CBD to foraging in the garden for Dandelions; it may take you on a new path of hope. Sometimes if I can feel myself getting anxious focusing on food in the hedgerow or preparing Kombucha makes me feel calmer like I'm contributing towards the solution.

Each chapter in this book is designed to have potential answers and nutrition may be the answer for you; the power of nature should not be underestimated.

In a nutshell:

- To survive; oat cakes, avocado, mango, banana, carrots raw vegetables (organic if possible) nuts and seeds, dark chocolate; plenty of fluids and honey in tea; if needed. Mix honey with cinnamon powder if you like it. Bulk order from wholefoodsonline.co.uk
- Replacement coffee with mineral rich chicory.
- If cooking; stir fry veg in coconut oil with fresh ginger and garlic, with rice noodles.
- Mash potato with pesto and any veg to go with it.
- Supplements, Vitamins B (B12 especially) vitamin C powder, Turmeric with black pepper;

- If you have IBS or stress associated bowl issues get a probiotic of at least 50 billion; use 'The Microbiome Solution' for guidance.
- Kombucha
- Forage from your garden; Dandelion leaves, Nettles clip with gloves and put in a pan washed with potatoes and add stock; this is a great tonic. Always make sure you collect plants from land that is not sprayed or contaminated.
- Juice grass with apples from your garden or an area where you know chemicals haven't been used. You may need to drain off the grass as this doesn't digest too well. A Masticator juicer is the best way to extract grass. Grass goes well with apple or oranges.
- Over time, look at the gut diets to eliminate leaky Gut or other depleting conditions like Candida and the recipes in Michael Mosley 'Clever Gut' and Robynne Chutkan's book 'The Microbiome Solution.

Plus also see Alternative medications sections

Foraging continued (*)

Plants And Us.

Someone said to me recently that there is no 'evidence' that plants heal and that is why our health system is modern pharmaceuticals because it is based on evidence. What is evidence then?

The whole of the plant kingdom has been researched, trialled, documented and passed between generations. The whole process to discover edible food, for example, may have cost a few lives and this 'evidence 'was passed down so we could distinguish poisonous plants.

The medical system was developed from plants but strangely enough when it emerged the clinical trials were never compared with its plant equivalent (see 'The 100 Year Lie' Fitzgerald.) The only comparison was placebo trials and so from there on in the 1930s this bible of information that had been carefully passed from generation to generation started to lose itself within a commercial system.

Interestingly enough in Leslie Taylor's book "The Healing Power of Rainforest Herbs' after curing herself of terminal cancer at age 27 with rainforest plants ,she comments;

"I didn't understand then (or now, really) is why they call chemotherapy and today's modern medicine "conventional medicine," and refer to herbal medicine as "alternative." My personal journey showed me that herbal medicine was much more conventional. It dates back literally centuries in time, with less than 100 year old pharmaceutical industry offering "alternatives" to plant medicine was much more effective than the "alternatives" conventional medicine offered me in my personal battle with cancer."(page 2)

She explains intricately why a plant cannot be assessed for its pharmaceutical value because of its multiple compounds so to be *"synthesized into a patentable drug it does not matter how active or* **beneficial."** It is, If the pharmaceuticals cannot profit from the plant it is not a viable option.

What is clear is that as we deplete the rain forests we also deplete the potential knowledge of plant medicine from the Shamans. Plants that can cure many diseases that are still unknown or ignored by modern medicine, but she makes clear that the CEOs, stockholders will receive the most benefit whilst the *"indigenous communities receive few, if any benefits.' (page 29)*

We know a scientific theory can turn on its head over a decade or even less and the wholesomeness of pharmaceutical on the market is not always determined because its full outcomes are not fully documented.

My nephew recently had a very serious adverse reaction to a trial injection. When I asked if it had been reported he replied 'no' and evidence continually shows (see Chapter 4) that these adverse affects reporting systems are significantly unused and unheard of by most people. So how can it be a wholly reliable system, If the results are very rarely made obvious and total outcomes just don't exist because of the poor reporting system it provides?

(*)https://digital.ahrq.gov/ahrq-funded-projects/electronic-support-public-health-vaccine-adverse-event-reporting-system

This in itself is not scientific because a vast part of the evidence does not exist. Many reports state that true side effect reporting only accounts for 1 to 10% of the real picture. (*)This is suitably convenient for an industry that has become profit led. In America the FDA (Food And Drug Administration) now is heavily sponsored **(45%)** by the very people who apply for regulation of their products; the pharmaceuticals. As a result there has been a significant decrease in the amount of time it takes a new drug to become available and drug withdrawal , due to adverse side effects, has increased. Thinks about that!

Russell Brand - The FDA FUNDED By The Big Pharma Companies It "REGULATES" – Is This Right? | Facebook

The famous plant healer Maurice Messegue in his beautiful book 'Of Plants And Men' notes

'I began to realize just how dangerous medicine can be when I hear of babies being treated for eczema with shots of cortisone, or infants being given barbiturates, I have no hesitation in calling it criminal follow. The study of medicine taught me, above all, the need for humility in medical work and the need to recognize that our surest knowledge is that we know nothing. So many times I have known patients go to three or four doctors, all capable and honest men, only to wind up with as many diagnoses as doctors. This is why I say that medicine is an art, not an exact science.'(107)

All the books about natural health Raymond shares with me are so eye opening and made me feel a faith in healing myself and working with nature. My time with him is always precious and therapeutic. I have recorded some of our sessions as I know his journey on this earth may be shorter than mine as he is 83 now, so I want to remember everything he has chosen to pass on to me.

Although dated, Messegue's story inspired me; it showed a healer that had the knowledge and instinct of treating each person individually with plants. He inherited this knowledge from his Father and his remedies and regular hand, footbaths and poultices fascinated me. One disease/disorder would require treating many physiological systems. Like modern medicine a cure is often not instant and takes few weeks of continual use to see positive results. Here for example he describes how he healed Schoum, an alcoholic 'Tramp' (his description) who was covered in eczema;

"I had reflected a great deal on Schoum's case and decided to focus my treatment on his liver and bowls, to rid them of all poisons; his kidneys, to stimulate them to eliminate the toxins in his body; his nerves, to subdue the itching; and his skin, to treat the scaly patches of eczema.

For his liver I relied mainly on artichoke....country dwellers used to treat jaundice most successfully with the roots of 'artichoke.' It is an effective cholagogue; it has considerable diuretic powers and the property of lowering the level of urea in the blood. As it will also cure certain skin infections of hepatic origin, for Schoum it was the miracle plant. I supplemented it with yarrow, cabbage leaf and thyme.

For his intestines I chose the charming, humble white hedge bindweed, such a modest little plant it often goes unnoticed but is nevertheless an excellent purgative....

For his nerves I chose lime blossom and hawthorn, the lovely 'whitethorn,' that Professor L.Binet in his books 'Le Plantes et la Sante des Hommes 'calls 'valerian of the heart.' It is one of the best anti spasmodic in existence, having none of the toxic effects of those chemical tranquillizers so freely indulged in today.

As a diuretic I used common broom – held in high repute since 1701 when it rid the Marshal Of Saxony of a dropsy that had defied the most skilful doctors of the day – and the flowers of meadow-sweet and the roots of couch-grass

Lastly to treat the eczematous I chose sage flowers and the leaf of great burdock, which my Father used to call 'scurf grass' and of which I mostly use the roots. This plant is considered one of the specific remedies for scaly and impetiginous eczema. I also included greater celandine, which is at once diuretic, purgative, cholagogue and narcotic and its successfully employed against ulcers and scurfy infections.'

Messegue cured Schoum as well as many others of severe painful acute conditions such as asthma, deformities, arthiritis . He became a threat to the medical practice who took him to court. His knowledge from his Father was an integral part of a French peasant community who were connected with nature and plants; both have become disconnected and for our own mental health we need to open up these gates. Plant treatments still need to be precise but results can be powerful.

Perhaps one day their resurgence will work alongside modern medicine to reunite this very undervalued gentle but effective system which is often so much more compromising and safe to over sensitive, over stimulated bodies. Have faith that as well as modern pharmaceuticals there are many alternative treatments for mental health which are equally as powerful but less destructive in their side effects. It is always worth consulting a professional for this and being consistent with dosage.

Helpful books and Links to this section (also at the end.)

The Microbiome Solution Robynne Chutkan

Hedgerow Medicine   Julie Bruton-Seal and Matthew Seal (merlin Unwin 2018)

The Lost Book of Herbal remedies by Nicole Apelian (Claude Davis 2021)

https://integrative-medicine.ca/magnesium-deficiency-mental-health/

The Clever Guts Diet Michael Mosley (Short Books 2017)

 Go to CBDUsersuk on facebook

The Thyroid Reboot by Kinsey Jackson

Also for Thyroid see Forefront Health

Sowing Seeds In The Desert by Masanabo Fukuoka

Of Plants And Men by Maurice Messegue

The Wild Wisdom of Weeds by Katrina Blair (Grass benefits)

Kombucha-Miracle Fungus The Essential Handbook Harald Tietze

 "The Healing Power of Rainforest Herbs' by Leslie Taylor

The 100 year Lie by Randall Fitzgerald

Suzanne Humphries Vitamin C powder
http://orthomolecular.org/resources/omns/v14n13.shtmlr;

Healthline.com; As always get advice and guidance and if pregnant check with your health professionals.

*The term 'neuroplasticity,' (another relatively new term over the last 2 decades) has started to fascinate scientists researching how stress affects our bodies but more importantly how the potential to change long term patterns of stress and thus physical responses are totally changeable. I will invite you to read Joe Dispenza's first- hand experience of coming out of a severe spinal injury in his amazing book "Evolve Your Brain," also pictured in the reference section. This holds good explanations and understanding of this term.

Next poem is not for the workers who helped and fully understood the pain I was in. Thank you. This poem is more critical of those who simply should not work with mentally afflicted people simply because of lack of empathy/ understanding which lead to further stigmas wrong decisions which translates into the sufferer as 'I am very ill, I will never get better, No-one understands, No-one is listening to me...' etc. It is important if you feel you are not being heard or listened to that you request another worker. The right therapist, the right support worker is out there for you and if you feel worse after a session, not better, that is a good indication that the person is not right for you. Andy and Agnes thank you for making me see this. It is really hard when you want to pull your head off your body and someone is explaining protocols and ticking boxes for their benefit not yours.

I might be 'mental' but show me some respect!

What led you to take up this role,

Did you think it was good karma,

Good for your soul?

(ha! I mock you as I feel you mock me!)

I observe your face with no expression

But I'll tell you for me

Each day is a lesson.

For I am a Mother, a daughter, a sister

Who is alone.

I lost my mind to Fear

And I am desperately trying to get home.

So don't tell me about

The protocol, some god given guideline

Decided in a clinical meeting

Because these words are just barriers

And distortions that to me, are more defeating.

And don't tell me how to behave

Because in these shoes you would understand

How I have to be brave.

I am getting the impression you look down on me

And like many people in this profession

Your curtness lacks, and there is no empathy.

You are good at ticking boxes and making your work look right

But in your clinical job; you do not know loneliness

And how frightened I will be tonight!

Chapter 10

<u>Who I have become; inner me, spirits, miracles and Simon.</u>

Part of me is writing this book with doubt that anyone will be interested, that doubt is a little girl who is still present, who I have come to know.

The new Morag knows me to be a very intelligent and loveable person who wants to help, but is not scared if no-one reads or doesn't like the poems and pictures which I have started to create, like a child exploring my curiosities.

The fear of rejection is no longer prominent, the need to be liked; gone. Why?

Because if I just got through that load of shit, I just don't give a fuck who likes me or not. I now have regard for myself and a passion for others to start the same journey of self love.

Finding myself hormonal or anxious (yes I still get anxious), or ill can set that little girl off and she can still take quite a seat in the house of Morag. If I'm tired or hungover or over eating I don't 'shoo' her away anymore, I sit with her and nurture her and let her have a good old 'paddy' till I've reassured her that the evidence is out there and it's all ok, and that if I walked through hell and lived to tell the tale then together we must have great strength because we both *invest and listen to the stable, the strong and the vulnerable aspect of ourselves; and that is our power*.

This breakdown, this depression, whatever it is ,try not to let anyone label it; it is not yours to keep. It is actually a terrible passage that will lead to your strength. If you understand the positives, you have got out of it and are prepared to look at yourself and your own vacuums it will have the opposite effect...as they say 'fall and you may fly.'

I could never believe it would be over but it is and here I am.

One of the most important people I met during my incapacitation as a human being gave me a necklace; it was made of local melted metal and was shaped like a daisy with a blue agate centre stone.

He told me that when I felt so awful to hold onto this daisy and know 'It will Pass.'

At that point he was the only light I had left...he was a healer named Simon who offered me his home when I was so terrified to be alone he offered me his caravan that became my sanctuary, (also see the next poem 'My Corner.')

His Reiki healing work is well known around the village he lives close to, but for me some of the healing didn't seem to work and I thought I was beyond anyone's help.

I had tried so many therapies and spent so much of money which I didn't have; my family had lent me money but nothing seemed to work.

Simon had a vision, and his vision was all I had left. Simon spoke to spirits....what a bizarre world I had found but I didn't care who he spoke to. He was kind and generous and could cope with my daunting presence which many had escaped.

He told me that when a friend had brought me to him a few months after I got sick he knew he was supposed to look after me. He had seen a very clear image of me in what he described as a blue/green costume running through water looking behind me at my son who was splashing me. I was laughing and I was well. The spirits were showing him that I would get better.

I used to sit in the corner of his caravan watching TV...I would turn up, sometimes in the morning after getting my son to school, in an exhausted state. He always took me in and gave me healing when he could.

When I had no hope left, I would cuddle up to Simon and ask about the vision. He would get frustrated but never retract. He would say, 'I am psychic; I've never been wrong with these visions.'

A year or so before this man would have been a stranger to me...I may never have met him if I hadn't got ill. Suddenly I was living with him (as friends only) half the time and when I wasn't with him I was ringing him. I am not sure how his patience with me continued but he is an exceptional person.

Two summers passed (not sure how I survived for that long) and Simon's vision had not come about. The vision was in the sunshine so I had assumed it took place in summer but sadly another Summer had gone and Autumn was drawing in the shorter days. I really thought I wouldn't be able to make it to the next summer and I was giving up hope.

Just after the new Psychiatrist that Helen endorsed (Dr K), a change of medication and Denise moved into my house, things were moving forward a little and small signs of improvement were showing.

I had been looking or watching out for that vision even though but nothing had happened like Simon stated. I actually owned a green/blue bikini but that wasn't to be the item of clothing that finally took its part in Simon's prediction.

I took Denise to the beach and I remember my head felt a bit clearer on that day and I felt some hope. I had another friend, Laurian, with me and I felt safe. It was a sunny September in 2016. I had forgotten my swim stuff and my son was playing in a rock pool with friends. I remember this alien feeling of perhaps happiness(?)...running through my tiny body. I pulled my t-shirt over my pants and started playing in the water. I splashed my son and he splashed me back, it was cold and I started to run, turning back I looked at my son and there it was in that moment; there was his vision.

I was still having some rough times so wondered if that had been it? Next time I visited Simon, I had a cup of tea and explained what had happened; I went to say I had forgotten my swimsuit and had a 'bluey/turquoise coloured top on'...I got to 'swimsuit and had a...' then **Simon finished my sentence with the exact** words 'a bluey/turquoise coloured top on.' I looked up and he was crying. I asked what the matter was he said 'I now know you are going to be well.' Despite his clear vision he had started to doubt my recovery as my fall had gone on for so long. After this event everything just got better and better.

I think I got some faith back in life and spirit after this. I was quite spiritual in my 20s being inspired by Neil Donald Walsh's book 'Conversations with God' amongst others such as The Celestine Prophecy which was popular at the time. Somehow I had lost this connection with life until now.

Here's an exert of my written memories of getting better and starting to feel life again and simply just 'Feel.'

'One day I am walking my dog to the beach...I live in a beautiful part of the world but when you lose yourself even Paradise can look bleak.

I know I am starting to get better, now my head still feels like it is stuffy and cloudy but there is hope.

There are lots of people on the beach catching the most of the remaining Autumn rays before Winter penetrates their hearts and they wrap themselves in sheepskin solitude.

There is a long driftwood tree trunk that has been put upright in the sand like a totem pole. It stands proud looking out to St Ives bay as rays of orange and red melt over tiny white houses.

I look out from the totem pole. I am vulnerable and yet brave. If there was more than me here right now we may be sitting round the pole feeling at one with each other, something which I had totally lost during these last two years.

These structures of rituals are special for human beings and indicate a past existence that was based on community, celebration and support; in other words connection.

I guess I am lucky. I still have my job and my son and I can walk a short way and feel the elements touch my skin as often as I like. I am rich in surroundings but when I was broken all this meant nothing. No matter which person advised that I should try to feel gratitude there was nothing but despair....

No one understands unless they have been in this skin. Some people find it hard to even talk about it once they are back here in this beautiful world, but I am and I do and I will.

Out of all those professionals **you are the expert and you are the brave one**.

So now after people have seen me fall and many have walked in the opposite direction I have an inner regard for the journey I survived.

Any misrepresentation of what happened to me over the past two years is no longer a worry; that is their world not mine. **My world was taken and this new one does not require their approval**. *As it states in the last poem, 'I was never at their court,' so how could I tell my story?*

My story is here now entwined and expressed in every word of this book; I have undone and rewoven the tapestry of the mentally afflicted. *That is the community or Totem pole I will grace myself with and may it reach up high and shine a light on our attitudes and complacencies around this subject.*

This is not an angry moment or a violin moment; it's a fact. **Those who experience severe mental health downfalls and breakdowns and survive are war heroes of the head**. *They deserve your respect,* not resistance and fear. Don't give them your advice; give them you, by trying to understand and be there for them if possible. All they need to hear is **'this will pass'** and the fact that you will be there for them until it does. Just listen, nurture and hold.

We can all race to charity events drink in hand, bidding for objects that make us feel we are helping a good cause. We can set up a direct debit in minutes to contribute towards helping getting us out of the atrocities that continue to plague these worlds, but can you give your time and kindness and just be with someone without expectations, knowing it will be tough and of no benefit to you? **This is charity.**

Tonight, after having a couple of days of anxiety which are getting fewer, I took the dog for a walk. My anxiety had eased and there in the sky were clear jewels like I had never seen them before. I feel part of their clarity.

Orange stripe close to the land; the Sun saying goodbye for today. I am thinking of Kate Bush's 'An Endless Sky of Honey' and 'Prologue Aerial,' each note absorbing into in my soul with a sense of renewal that I have come to know happy again.

The news does not matter. The TV does not matter. I have seen a thousand sunsets but tonight I feel so lucky to be looking at this sky. I would never have known this gratitude if I hadn't been to hell.

Hold on my child...it is your child who is crying the one who hasn't been listened to all this time. Visualise him and hold him, nurture him; tell him it will all be ok because it will.

The other day I was walking with my partner (a new relationship about a year and a half after my recovery) he was being belligerent in a funny way; whatever he was saying I said back to him.

"Matthew you know how intolerant I am of people since having my breakdown!"

It was a humorous moment and we both laughed. However what was funny was that I was referring to the breakdown almost affectionately as 'mine' (which I don't usually do) and there it was a gratitude that because of it I choose who I hang out with.

I no longer need to carpet bomb social occasions to get just the right friends and the right partners. Here I am this is me, take it or leave it. Ironically, I lost a lot of friends because of the breakdown. Now, post breakdown, the slate is cleaned and all these interesting exciting characters keep coming into my life.

It is the opposite of 'will they like me?'' I am' and then I choose. As a result my friends are less in quantity but so much more in depth, richness and support. In other words I know myself and trust my judgement to choose who will enhance my life and give me what I need.

I am kind and empathic, so this is what I expect from someone else and then our relationship will flow and flourish.

Let me make it clear this is no reflection on anyone that couldn't help me it just wasn't their time for each of us in our life we all have to learn kindness and humility. As the spiritual teachers say these actions vibrate at a much higher frequency or even Neil Donald Walsh who believes **we already unconsciously know who we are. Our lifetime is about expressing it through these actions.**

My Corner

(Dedicated to Simon who I owe my life to.)

How do you show gratitude

When I didn't want to eat

You gave me Food.

When there was no hope

And I stood on the edge

You passed me a rope

And said 'Come back

On this throne!'

I will make you safe

And show you How

You don't have to be alone.

When no-one had time

To give

You stopped the clocks

And said 'I will wait

Till you can live

Till you feel alive'

You offered me this safe Corner

So I could survive.

Chapter 11

The Bridge

My recovery involved coming to terms with what had happened to me, whether chemicals had worsened the situation or not, it was still necessary to explore the jigsaw of experience that had made up my life.

This helped me scan the emotional patterns that helped me understand some of the self-sabotage I had operated in my life. When I say self sabotage, I am really not holding any blame to the sufferer.

I thought I had really grown into a more aware self-loving person, but we should always be mindful that our learning is never complete and then we can continue to grow.

I still held my counseling sessions once a week with Andy, who had worked around my illness, and found the right therapeutic approach that suited me and he had done it for a minimal charge.

He offered me hope, acceptance and understanding about myself that helped unfold and make sense of the crazy journey I had found myself on.

In recovery I felt elated, relieved, frightened and physically exhausted; having these points of contact was important.

One day during my recovery Andy said we would try an inner child meditation. I lay on the couch and shut my eyes. **I want to say I felt like I was humoring Andy; I didn't think this exercise would work for me.**

Andy asked me to go to a place that I felt calm and relaxed; it took me a while to think, and then I remembered a woodland in Devon behind my Mom's house. It was accessed from a beautiful field scattered with native oaks and sweet horse chestnut looking across to views along the River Dart. I always felt hopeful and boundless watching life go by here.

When I walked into the woods from this stretch the trees enclosed around a little brook and a bridge. It was on the bridge I stood. I was then asked to let 'the Emma of my childhood' come to the bridge so I could talk, embrace or play with her, or whatever I felt comfortable with.

What happened next was unexpected; a beautiful but vulnerable little girl around two years of age approached me with a short dress and a knitted nappy/pair of pants (yes my Mom used to crochet us pants!) I recognized the bowl haircut of white that shone in the speckled light of the sun that streamed through the trees.

I felt uncomfortable, **I couldn't look her in the eyes, I felt quite emotional. I may have felt some anger towards her. Whatever I felt I couldn't pick her up, hold her or play with her; I didn't hate her either. I felt sad and as Andy was gently telling me to embrace her I was feeling guilty for not being able to do this.**

I remained silence in the meditation as Andy let me continue, unbeknown to him I was uncomfortable with this meeting in my head but I didn't want to stop. I was surprised how cut off I was from this little stranger.

It broke my heart that I could cut off from her. I'd ignored her for so long and knowing I had come so far, I thought this task would be fairly easy.

I wanted to desperately help this girl; after all she was me. Why couldn't I love her? Out of desperation suddenly, I am not sure whether I consciously did this, **but my son came into the scene, and he started playing with the little me**.

I felt like I was cheating in the task but it made me smile to see the immediate love and acceptance my son showed her. He didn't falter and immediately she was so comfortable, and there we were the three of us working it out, or at least I was.

Andy found this interesting, and when I got home I continued this meditation until I was comfortable to meet the little girl on my own at The Bridge and give her a hug.

It is still work in progress, but what did it mean?

After all the work and discovery I had opened about myself, here I was trying hard to love my inner child. Firstly, I realized that for whatever reason my intuition and some of the work I had done with Tessa Goldhawk through hypnotherapy had made me realise that I had been very vulnerable in my life, not only because of my Father as an alcoholic but the situation I was born into; an unexpected arrival that may have caused additional stress, to my already struggling parents.

Whilst coming off the medication (which has always given me vivid dreams) and during my recovery I had a dream of being a small body like a baby in a cot terrified because she was unsafe. The screams I was screaming in the dream fed a terror I have never known. No-one was answering my calls and it seemed that this terror was never going to end. My head felt like it would explode. I awoke with a jolt, so pleased to slowly come round and realize I was dreaming. My other analysis of this situation is that the trauma had arisen from my unconscious and by coming to the surface had dissipated. (*)

(*)Strangely my son had a similar experience when his Dad left him to sleep in his car as a baby whilst he went to get fish and chips. His screams were so loud that people ran into the fish and chip shop to inform Dad who came quickly out to calm him. Was my son carrying my trauma? My son has not forgotten this and that is good because we discuss it and go over it so it can stream through his subconscious and release itself. We also re enact it in our heads and turn it into a funny event. Next we are going to get fish and chips from the same shop with a hope to re write its history in my son's head.

My Mother had a tough time when she brought me into the world, so who knows whether she occasionally put me in a room on my own so she could cope? It could be a range of traumas but this might also explain why when I got ill I became terrified of being on my own in the house. This seemed to correlate to one of the most terrifying dreams I had during my recovery.

More importantly did I need to trace this trauma back? Would I ever find out what had happened to me as a baby if anything? Do we need to trace our unconscious traumas? Sometimes yes, but for me learning to meet that little girl and play with her on my own was paramount to understanding me and my self-worth.

This in itself is healing and again not hiding how I originally felt about that little girl but feeling those feelings without guilt, then letting them flow and disseminate.

The other important learning lesson from this was our children. **Children as Phil Borges said, like their elders are closer to the spirit world than us, and whilst providing boundaries for them, we also need to allow their creativity and playfulness evolve.** I realized that my son had helped that transition from me feeling uncomfortable with my inner child to me learning to love her.

My own child had taken me on a journey to self-love, and in everyday life I realized he brings out humor and magical parts that I buried a long time ago before I had him. His openness and acceptance, like many children, had immediately accepted and embraced that child; and that for me was just beautiful.

Despite my desperate false attempts to show him I was ok when I was ill my son was the only one who wanted to be near me. Everyone else found it difficult; **but his heart (though anxious) knew that I was in trouble and even if he suffered, he needed to be in my presence to know I was OK.**

So if you have children don't always block them from your suffering, allow them to be playful and listen to the lesson they teach us as adults; **bringing up a child is not a one way journey.**

Finally I want to say within all the pain we have experienced, as Elanor Longdon so eloquently put about her memories of those who have harmed her; *"**Their memories grow pale and faint in comparison to those that helped.**"*

If we can see our lives as a journey and not get stuck in the pain we will become free from those events and traumas that have held us a prisoner for so long.

As a result of what I have written in 'The Bridge' **this book is of course dedicated to my son Sebby as is inspired by the song** 'Little Giant' by Roo Panes.

A Tiny Poem For Your Big Heart

(to my son)

Words are important

So don't waste them

If you lose me

Do not ever live in my shadow

My wish is that

You live in my light

Weep and grieve

By all means

Then let it pass

Whatever sufferings

Before I passed

This has passed

Gone.

Do not go over and over it

And become it

For now I am free

In my light

Forever with you

Do not live in my shadow

Do not live in shadow

Live in your light

Live in my light

Without fear

Do not fear those with bigger words than you

For they cannot hold you

Unless you let them

They hold those words as security

For they have none

And you are free

Walk this earth with a big heart

My little giant

Do not lose your unique radiance to loss;

there is no loss.

For I am here

Always

Beating in every

beat of you.

On our adventures once again! 😊 2019

Love this boy, love his energy...Lock into your children's energy in lockdown stay away from the fear rhetoric..build dens, bounce around like a monkey to Joe Wicks; be a child, be you in the moment, learn from them..their world hasn't failed: ours has!

Chapter 12

<u>Perceptions Of Mental Health</u>

Let me tell you about despair because I know you are in it. Let me tell you there is reasoning and hope behind all suffering. My Angel, open your heart and know there are souls who will hold your hand and carry you through this.

I couldn't work out whether to give capital letters to Mental and Health because I don't want readers to feel like it is an impingement on their world but I want everyone to notice that it needs attention.

Someone said to me recently that she found the term 'mental health problem' offensive like people with mental health issues were a problem; I get this. In the same way saying 'unemployed Mother' really infers that Mothers are not contributing towards society whilst they are actually nurturing a human being; one of the greatest honors we should behold.

There are a few spiritual warriors in this fragmented world that are prepared to carry us through this pain. There are some though that spend their lives studying others to improve and understand the human soul. Photographer Phil Borges is one of these.

Phil studies and photographs tribes, his work is inspirational and beautiful but his observations about mental health in these tribes is phenomenal.

He notes that survival of tribes purely depend on plants as well as their own ingenuity; something our modern world has lost. Tribes are about consciousness, rebirth and connection. **The elders are seen as closer to the spirit world as are children who have just come from spirit.**

How beautiful that they always seem to gravitate towards each other in the tribal community; another connection that has been lost in our modern existence.

Mental health within tribal communities is often **seen as death of the old self and rebirth** of the new, which I feel is exactly what happened to me.

If this is a process (as Borges suggests) then chemicals, as a solution, could put this process into a realm of numbness that will never get the process realized.

Many long- term mental health conditions occur in teenage years, particularly if young people start to hear voices. Borges observed in some tribes the older communities scoop the troubled youngster up and shelter them in their company, knowledge and nurture. More importantly their mental health 'issues' are not seen as a 'problem' or an inconvenience; they are seen as a **gift or a journey.**

When we are looking at mental health from this angle, it is so clear that in the West within **our fragmented lives we separate the elders, the working people and children from each other** in our everyday lives. It is easy to see how mental health does become a problem, an inconvenience against the obsession of money growth rather than spiritual development.

Perhaps one day we will honor those who suffer for they are all on a journey for us.

Borges also brought my attention to the TED talk that went viral from the beautiful soul Elanor Longden.

Longdon started to hear voices in her head when she began studying at an English University. The harmless voices became more animated and harmful as she became diagnosed as a Schizophrenic.

More analysis and more pharmaceutical treatment led her to harsh reactions, reaching a pinnacle where she physically tried to drill a hole in her head to get the voices out. Her brave and beautiful speech testifies to her survival and reframing mental health from long held perceptions.

Although I did not hear voices, listening to Longden talk about her survival and awakening from this hell were so comparative with my own experience it melted my heart. I was quite emotional when I watched the talk.

She describes that **'whilst she died in that place the person that awoke was 'a survivor.'**

She did come off all the medication (as I have) and got away from the continual diagnosis and looked towards people that told her that her recovery was 'totally possible;' does this sound familiar?

In fact, Longden then graduated in a Masters of Psychology and she learned from her own experience **that the voices in her head were just symptoms or cries from unresolve traumas and experiences.** She had shut down, yet the kindness she received through her recovery compared to those that had harmed or hurt her *"grew pale and faint in comparison to those that helped me."*

So how does our current society help mental health?

When we become fragmented in society, i.e.when we dismantle community we also become dismantled in our knowledge. We can pay for education to get a 'better service' but this means it puts a limitation on who will be educated.

So, if you have money, your intellectual intelligence does not have to be tested too much, if you want to study. On the other hand, if you haven't got money (regardless of how intelligent and what life experience you may possess) your ability to study will depend on the amount of money you have. This is another example of fragmentation.

Certainly, without saying wealthy people will not have empathy or be kind, *useful people in society need to have empathy, which often means they will probably have experienced pain themselves. So, making opportunities for people who just have one credit; wealth may mean they have limited understanding of suffering? You don't always have to experience suffering but to be able to connect with people suffering and surviving is a great qualification and skill.*

This is so apparent after our recent 'pandemic' where the pillars of society that we could not do without were the least acknowledged in what we call 'status' and poorly paid, and most people who go into this profession are not wholly motivated by income but more a passion to connect and help others.

Some people have natural born empathy even though they have had pretty good lives; they really do and I met some of those people during my journey. Largely, individuals who train to be Psychiatrists, Doctors always wanted to help people, but they were born within a system based on money and that is one of the main solution techniques they can become indoctrinated with.

Just as many governments are funded by institutions; and it is these institutions and corporations they come to represent, instead of the people that voted for them. In the same way medical staff are influenced and pulled on a string by big pharmaceuticals who actually pay (via the government) for any medical procedure intervention undertaken. That is right; when did we ever agree to that unethical model?

More shocking is that many of the politicians have personal share investment in the pharmaceuticals. I on the other hand have to declare ANY gift given to me by my clients in my job. *Can you see the hypocrisy in all of this?*

This is just another example of increasing fragmentation and that strengthening and empowering communities is paramount to a creating a society.

You may be saying 'this is political,' well yes it is; read the whole of this book my friend and what you will realise is that we are a symbiotic entity; governments influence people as do media.

It would be nice if you don't have to give a shit about the total pressure your government and society has put on you when you fall apart, because, when you do, time stops, **and there you are on the bottom step of society. It is then you realize what those who suffer the most are offered the least; particularly when it comes to mental health.**

Unless you have a large wedge of wealth, your home and money can deplete at great speed. I was incredibly lucky to have a local authority job and a low mortgage and that is how I didn't end up on the streets.

Here at this low point, you will see the cracks and get caught between them in a lonely frightening place caused by cuts and bureaucracy in one of the richest nations.

Imagine some of the poorer countries and how frightening it may be for someone to find their mental health decline. Unless of course within that poverty there is a greater sense of community that open their arms to those who are afflicted?

I am sure the answer is a mixed bag of heartfelt and horror, but either way mental health needs to be universally addressed and the wealthier nations should hold their heads in shame for not investing in dynamic community-based systems.

In a 15-minute appointment, pharmaceuticals were thrown at me but no time to monitor or care for my condition and whilst metaphorically crawling in the dark I miraculously found angels; they do exist.

The sadness is for those who lose everything financially and emotionally and end up homeless, or off the cliff; all they may have needed was SNCS (safety, nuture, structure and connection) and not to be judged.

The destructive nature of our world will make this difficult to find, and this book is asking those around the hurt to nurture, and protect, and help recovery. Love and care even though small can grow till it reaches the heights that can be poured back into the planet, **because she too is sick.**

Right now, we are so far off where we need to go. We need to get to John O' Groats but are nearly at Land's End. Kind but powerful actions of love could create a U turn.

Constraints around money and medicine do not help people who fall by the wayside, but it doesn't mean we cannot start community and nurture from our own backyards.

Start reconnecting; remember a bad experience with friends and family who are broken will also take you through your own self-development, especially when they recover because it will have been your journey as well as theirs.

If you can help someone who is falling then create them a world they can cope with. You won't want to be there all the time, believe me. Even if you are family living in the house; include other people into their daily structure. It will be boring, tiring and quite frankly fucking hard but if you offer what you can, half a day a week, an evening perhaps?

Write them out a timetable this will be gold dust to start a potential solution in aiding them back to health.

Try not to start the all too familiar mantras of "I just can't cope anymore." "I haven't got the time.". "She got herself into this, she needs to sort it out..." "It's not my responsibility." "Hasn't she got family... "**Don't talk yourself out of it**, Connect, ask people, *create a community that works for them and that you can handle too.*

Be brave because to give enriches our spirit.

Let us all try contributing to the broken mental state of the planet; once you engage community you start to move. Our own fragmentation is one of suffering. Let's help create access, better facilities for mental health with a whole new perspective.

Let's view those who have fallen to be on a journey that will make them a better person in our society. **Let's look at our society and not just our own individual bubbles of wealth and want.**

Start a project; lobby the government, talk to people, be kind and show compassion always. Our true state is to connect and nurture not to divide.

There are many beautiful kind people in this world now doing it. If it helps try to slow your life down and get off the eternal rollercoaster of ego desires; it will not give you happiness. Protect your own mental health and let's start creating a new world for those who suffer.

There is lockdown to consider which wasn't even an element when I started writing this book.

The longer we lockdown for the more mental health and disconnection we create. The other side to this is that we are so desperate to get out of lockdown we become more vulnerable to control.

FB post during Covid 19:
A lot of you know I had nearly 2 years of severe anxiety and depression I thought I would never get out of it but I did. When you are not in control of your body and you haven't slept for weeks, you become in a different place. Severe depression and anxiety are very different from suffering from the odd bout of feeling flat /low or having small episodes of anxiety. It hits you like an avalanche and changes your life rapidly. Some people think suicide is selfish. This is a strange concept as they have no understanding of the illness that takes hold. People who experience this often find themselves judged in a way that no physical illness would ever warrant.

As you lose more and more control the thoughts that become prominent are 'I won't survive this anyway the sleeplessness etc so I must take control of the situation' and/or 'make it easy for everyone else as I am affecting their lives because of course it won't end.' It feels like it won't end but it does!

In the midst of my hopelessness, I remember advice coming through by text like 'Don't let anxiety rule your life...'I mean 'No shit Sherlock!'

I felt people were angry with me for being such a fuck up. I also felt as a Mother I had let my son down so badly. Luckily, he can't remember. But please don't put your frustrations onto those suffering when you have no understanding of how out of control they feel. Advice like this does not help; time and kindness and making them feel safe do. I am trying to say please don't judge anyone in these hard times if you have no understanding of being in their skin.

If your anxiety is bad there are many options both medical, herbal and therapeutic; but you must have people by your side when you take these as some can make you worse so there are risks and monitoring is vital. The first anti-anxiety/ depression drug you take may not suit you everyone is different avoid long term use of Benzos and Zopiclone. Some of the alternatives are also powerful and generally have less side effects but whatever works do whatever you have to do to get some sleep and back on a functional platform.

Our NHS and mental health services are a skeleton system to what they were; believe me I know this I was told often 'we just don't have the resources' It was a miracle I survived. I have completed a book about this journey to help people look at mental health in a more open, kinder way. I am saddened that we don't have mid-range mental health hospitals in our community as there used to be.

In the last month I know of several teenagers with mental health issue two of them have committed suicide. I also know of two adults who have taken their own lives; one a parent. Many people have died without their families by their side.

I know of two people who are not able to feed themselves and risk losing their homes because they fell through the furlough nets. Many people with mental health problems and dementia are in hospital now, scared because their loved ones aren't with them, policy says 'no' but humanity should say yes; there is no risk if done properly. Adults have not been able to attend their children's funerals or children their parents. Why have people dogmatically followed such tripe!

In Cornwall there have been about 276 deaths from Covid since this began over a year ago. An average mortality across the UK reaches on average about 600,000 a year. I just want to put things in perspective for you and to say to those out there who are feeling alone or fearful or who have lost their jobs and are spiralling reach out for help try and set up a structure, keep your world small. Do not watch the news; there are many kind people in this world. Try not to give up but I will never judge you if you do.

*<u>Lockdown;</u> When we went into Lockdown, initially the whole country was anxious. It was my trigger being alone. I expected to go into anxiety and awaited this unwanted visitor. She never came and I realised I had shed a skin and this was my true self. If anyone had learned about survival and loneliness I had. I was an expert, **never mind about being 2 metres from me; most people didn't want to be within 2 miles of me** and the thing is I didn't care what anyone thought of me I was simply just me. It had taken a few decades to get there but I had done it!

I wonder whether pandemics are part of our imbalance we have with nature and ourselves; this poem reflects this. Hold strong everybody and get back to yourselves. You can do this; you have this I know you do. You are so much more powerful than you think.

Lockdown (December 2020)

How long have we been in lockdown from ourselves?
This lockdown, briefly allowed the birds to sing.

A glimpse; a key perhaps?

Whist fearful others stripped the shelves

Embodiment of progress. More stripping by machine, by bombs. And here we stand in self-made deserts and lost songs. Looking to invest our money to take away the pain

From our hearts and wrongs.

Imbalances nature imbalance body and mind. So tech savy, but so far behind.

Mr Fukuoka I'm sorry we didn't follow your plans. 'A Giant Octopus,' you said 'Congratulating itself whilst chewing off its own legs' How long till we have exhausted and drank the very last dregs?

Then pandemics arrive and we fill the oceans with masks and paper plates. Wondering why we can't survive

How long have we been in lockdown? How long my child? I have been broken. But now I am awake. I no longer fear your lies. I am part of the unspoken

Speaking; this is our time

Chapter 12a

<u>*A Note to Parents; the simple secret to good parenting.*</u>

Aristotle said 'Give Me a Child Until he is 7 and I will show you the man.'

When children are young as they are learning, their brains operate in much slower waves (mainly Delta and Theta) this allows them to grow and sleep. It also allows them to **absorb.** *The rational reasoning part of the brain (the pre frontal cortex) is not in full swing till age 7 plus, so we can see why Aristotle made this statement. Their physical and emotional building blocks are open to the foundations of their life; and that comes mostly from their parents or carers.*

If you tell a child indirectly, they are not good enough "You can't have sweets because you have been naughty.' **They won't hear that they can't have sweets they will hear they are naughty**.

If you are told constantly, you are naughty or not good enough or too loud all the time, children absorb this.

Now this is not to say children shouldn't have boundaries but the conversation is very different. **Don't label but invite them to explore.**

E.g. If you break that object how will that affect someone else?' i.e. 'Mommy will not be able to buy another one, so you won't have anything to play with.' **You are inviting them to understand the effects of their actions rather than labelling them as 'useless', 'stupid' or 'not good enough.'**

This is a distinct difference I still do with my son. It becomes a conversation and if he becomes unreasonable you can bet your bottom dollar that he will go away and come back and say "Mom I'm really sorry that wasn't good behaviour!' **Can you see the difference he is observing his behaviours and not him.**

No one is anything, 'naughty 'useless' 'messy' 'spoilt' they behave a certain way because of a circumstance and yes children will want in those moments of frustration. Point out their behaviour and how it affects others and don't put a label upon them.

Even though I was much loved the words from my Nan and Mom were 'useless' and 'messy.' It was reinforced and I just acted the role.

What it meant, along with the trauma I experienced is there was a ceiling on what I could achieve because **I just wasn't good enough** *(see Chris Duncan's work in Chapter 9.)*

Affirming thoughts and trauma probably boiled over into an anxiety that could have been triggered medically or simply from becoming a parent which is a huge 'trigger milestone' for many.

Either way as a parent now I am firm, not 'wishy washy'. I am still the pack leader in the dynamics because children need that strength.

I do choose my battles (every parent knows that!) but I point out behaviour and side effects of such actions. I choose this rather than label or umbrella a child in a negative category because I want them to be an open human being"

Just to note though I am not perfect. I lose my temper, I sometimes feel when I am tired, I lack boundaries etc and here is the next important thing, **If I misbehave I am prepared to say to my son I am wrong. I am prepared to say sorry, e.g.** *"I am really sorry I just lost my temper; I am really tired and am worried about Nanny.'*

Can you see what I just did then not only did I say sorry I showed my son that I was not my emotions and was observing why I would behave like that. My son often says 'that's ok I'm sorry too. I think I was being a bit rude.' He was **being** *a bit rude* **but he wasn't rude.**

Explore these emotions with each other, then your children will become empathic gods and goddesses in this world and you will be able to set them free mentally and emotionally with great confidence.

I said at the beginning of this book 'in your imperfections lies your perfection' and that is exactly what this is about. Most importantly listen to their words and how they see the world they are on a different brain dynamic and time zone to you and they can become your greatest mindfulness teachers.

Love to all of you on your journey. You can only see your true light when it is dark my friend and I hope this journey will be your steps to recovery. We are all connected and you are definitely not alone.

References; *All references or studies / evidence are right under the comments I make associated with this but here is a quick reference to the main books/ talks I mentioned as well as a visual reference for easier use.*

Chapter 1 and General

https://www.itv.com/news/2018-12-21/military-personnel-veterans-suicides-mental-health-ptsd

Claire Weekes 'Self-help for your nerves."

'First, We make The Beast Beautiful' Sarah Wilson Penguin 2018

Chapter 4

A world without antidepressants: the new alternatives to prescription pills (telegraph.co.uk) and watch the amazing film **'Fantastic Fungi'**

Chapter 5

Breath 'The New Science of Lost Art by James Nestor

WimHoff https://www.youtube.com/watch?v=0BNejY1e9ik

https://www.youtube.com/watch?v=8GgAoZUYAvY

Chapter 8 The Spiritual Way

The Microbiome: How to Talk to Your 2 Million Genes - Deepak Chopra™

https://www.deepakchopra.com/book/total-meditation/

The Power of Now Eckhart Tolle

You're Not Broken by Christopher Michael Duncan

Donna Eden www.edenmethod.com

Nutrition; Chapter 9

The Microbiome Solution by Robynne Chutkan

The Thyroid Reboot by Kinsey Jackson (Paleoplan LLC 2020)

https://integrative-medicine.ca/magnesium-deficiency-mental-health/

The Clever Guts Diet   Michael Mosley (Short Books 2017)

 Hedgerow Medicine   Julie Bruton-Seal and Matthew Seal (Merlin Unwin 2018)_

The Wild Wisdom of Weeds   Katrina Blair (Grass benefits)

Kombucha-Miracle Fungus The Essential Handbook by Harald Tietze

The 100 year Lie Randall Fitzgerald

Of Men And Plants by Maurice Messegue (Weidenfeld & Nicolson 1972) ISBN 0 297 99495 6

The Healing Power Of Rainfoest Herbs by Leslie Taylor (Square One 2005)

The Lost Book of Herbal Remedies Nicole Apelian (Davis 2020)

Go to **CBD Usersuk** on facebook

Suzanne Humphries Vitamin C powder
http://orthomolecular.org/resources/omns/v14n13.shtmlr;

Tulsi; https://www.ncbi.nlm.nih.gov/pmc/articles/PMC4296439/

https://www.webmd.com/vitamins/ai/ingredientmono-1101/holy-basil

https://www.healthline.com/health/food-nutrition/basil-benefits

https://www.parkinsonsresource.org/news/articles/holy-basil-to-beat-stress-and-sleep-better/

A Compromised Generation by Beth Lambert. Sentient 2010

Films; Feel Good and Fascinating

Fantastic Fungi on Netflix

My Teacher The Octopus on Netflix

Further Development

The Mind Illuminated: A Complete Meditation Guide Integrating Buddhist Wisdom and Brain Science for Greater Mindfulness By Matthew Immergut (Author) Jeremy Graves (Contributor)

When Everything Changes, Change Everything by Neal Donald Walsh Mar 01,

Evolve Your Brain: The Science of Changing Your Mind by Joe Dispenza,

Sowing Seeds in the Desert: Natural Farming, Global Restoration, and Ultimate Food Security by Masanobu Fulkuoka

Talks

Elanor Longden 'I hear Voices' TED talks 2013

Phil Borges 'Psychosis or Spiritual Awakening?' (Tedtalks)

Lisa Miller 'Despair and Isolation'

Eckhart Tolle; any podcast

Deepak Chopra Abundance/ Health and Hope 21-day meditations

Internet; Mosaicscience.com

Hair

My hair was white
Bowl cut ready to ignite
Joy little spirit
Shine a light.

Then when I was a bit older
(I thought I was blonde)
Till someone described
'Mousey;' like a pond!

Sun struck too
I highlighted it
To be cool
for you
Till the fight to stay bright
stopped.

I became dark locked
Like my Mom
Realising that middle age
Had come.
I waited for thinning
And grey
Like part of me had left
Or gone away.
Nothing of the sort
Arose.

I felt a thick strong mane
Wind swept and full
Ready
For your retort.
Long but shaven
my experience to strength
then Warrior.
I started to see
the lies.
My light remained
And shone into your dark
Disguise.

And for my Mother
And all those that fight.
Through their trauma
This mane
She is a lion.
For one paw
Placed on you
Will dissolve
Deceit.

And you know this
Running.
I feel your fear
Footsteps...
For she is coming.

Help
Samaritans

Telephone: **116 123 (24 hours a day, free to call)**
Email: **jo@samaritans.org**
Website: **https://www.samaritans.org**

Provides confidential, non-judgemental emotional support for people experiencing feelings of distress or despair, including those that could lead to suicide. You can phone, email, write a letter or in most cases talk to someone face to face.

Mind Infoline

Telephone: 0300 123 3393 (9am-6pm Monday to Friday) or text 86463
Email: info@mind.org.uk
Website: www.mind.org.uk/information-support/helplines

Mind provides confidential mental health information services.

With support and understanding, Mind enables people to make informed choices. The Infoline gives information on types of mental health problems, where to get help, drug treatments, alternative therapies and advocacy. Mind works in partnership with around 140 local Minds providing local mental health services.

Rethink Mental Illness Advice Line

Telephone: 0300 5000 927 (9.30am - 4pm Monday to Friday)
Email: advice@rethink.org
Website: http://www.rethink.org/about-us/our-mental-health-advice

Provides expert advice and information to people with mental health problems and those who care for them, as well as giving help to health professionals, employers and staff. Rethink also runs Rethink services and groups across England.

Saneline

Telephone: 0300 304 7000 (4:30pm-10:30pm)
Website: www.sane.org.uk/what_we_do/support/helpline

Saneline is a national mental health helpline providing information and support to people with mental health problems and those who support them.

The Mix

Telephone: 0808 808 4994 (11am-11pm, free to call)
Email: Helpline email form
Crisis Support: Text 'THEMIX' to 85258.
Website: www.themix.org.uk/get-support

The Mix provides judgement-free information and support to young people aged 13-25 on a range of issues including mental health problems. Young

people can access the The Mix's support via phone, email, webchat, peer to
peer and counselling services.

ChildLine

Telephone: 0800 1111
Website: www.childline.org.uk

ChildLine is a private and confidential service for children and young people up to the age of nineteen. You can contact a ChildLine counsellor for free about anything - no problem is too big or too small.

Side by Side

Website: https://sidebyside.mind.org.uk/about

Side by Side is an online community where you can listen, share and be heard. Side by Side is run by Mind.

SHOUT

Shout is the UK's first 24/7 text service, free on all major mobile networks, for anyone in crisis anytime, anywhere. It's a place to go if you're struggling to cope and you need immediate help.

Text: 85258
Website: https://www.giveusashout.org/

NHS England IAPT (Improving Access to Psychological Therapies)

If you're based in England, you can use webpage to find and refer yourself to mental health services in your area.

Website: https://www.nhs.uk/service-search/find-a-psychological-therapies-service/

- Veterans' mental health charity Combat Stress is available 24 hours a day on 0800 138 1619 for veterans and their families, 0800 323 444 for serving personnel and their families, via text on 07537 404719, or through their website.
- Veterans' charity SSAFA is available on 0800 731 4880 or through their website.

- The Government's Veterans' Gateway offers advice and help for veterans seeking support and can be contacted on 0800 802 1212 or through the website

- Rock 2 Recovery - which helps veterans suffering from stress and their families - can be contacted on 01395 220072 Monday to Friday between 9am and 4pm, emailed at Support@rock2recovery.co.uk or through their website.

- Support | Man Down Cornwall (mandown-cornwall.co.uk)

THE INTERNATIONAL BESTSELLER
THE POWER OF
NOW
ECKHART TOLLE
JOE DISPENZA, D.C.
What the Bleep Do We Know!?
EVOLVE
your
BRAIN
The Science of
Changing Your Mind
Foreword by Amit Goswami, Ph.D.
A Complete Meditation Guide
Integrating Buddhist Wisdom and Brain Science for Greater Mindfulness
THE
MIND
LLUMINATED
CULADASA (JOHN YATES PhD)
MATTHEW IMMERGUT PhD WITH JEREMY GRAVES
NEALE DONALD WALSCH
Conversations
with God
book 1
An uncommon dialogue
THE INTERNATIONAL BESTSELLER

HEDGEROW MEDICINE
Herbal Remedies
JULIE BRUTON-SEAL
& MATTHEW SEAL
THE HANDMADE APOTHECARY
the forager handbook
A GUIDE TO THE EDIBLE PLANTS OF BRITAIN
of Weeds
KATRINA BLAIR
MILES IRVING

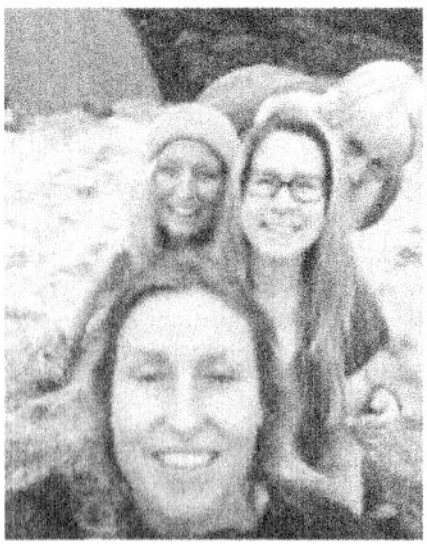
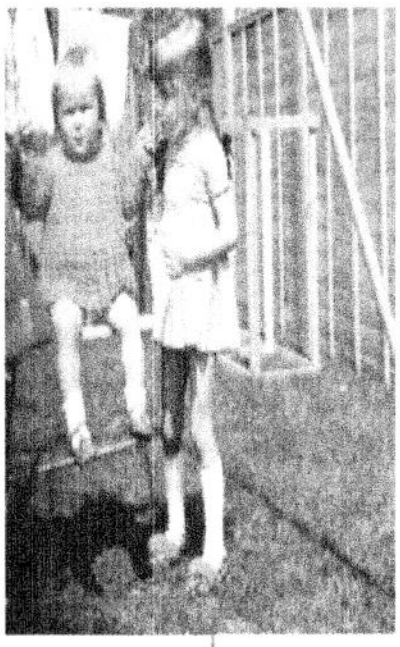
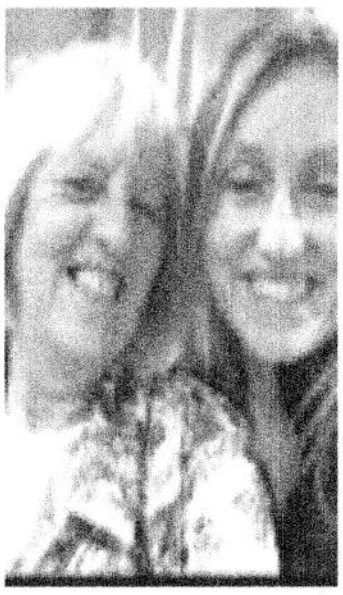
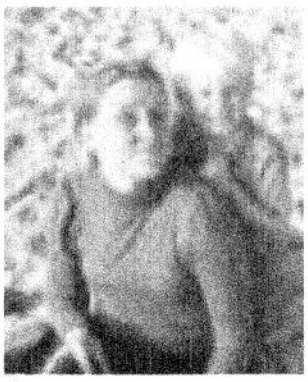
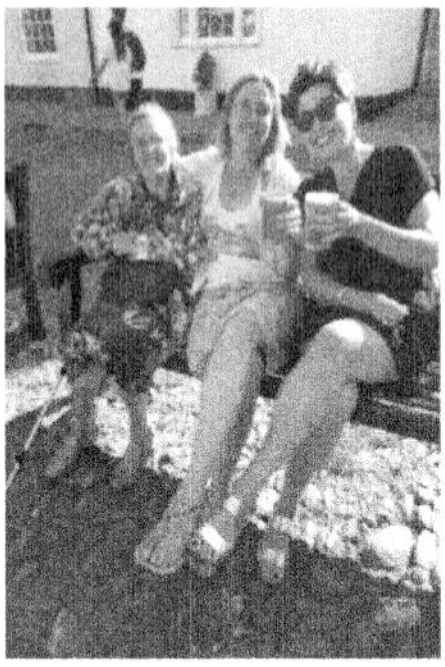
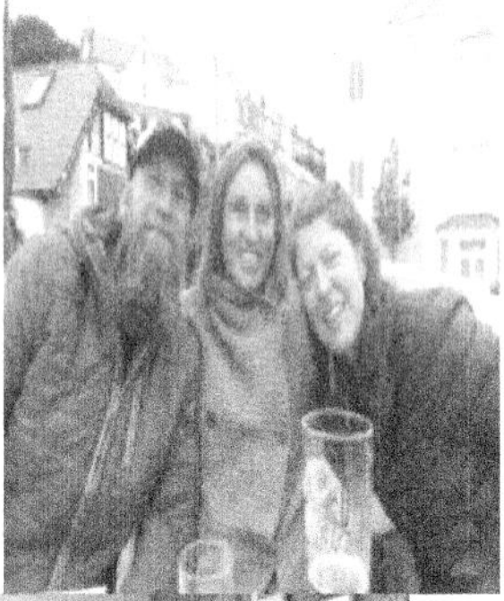
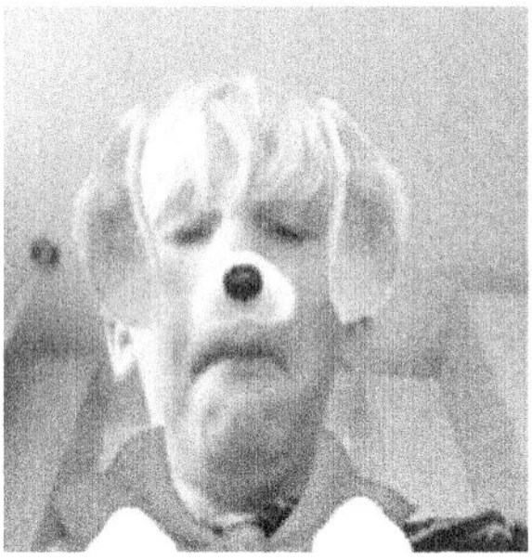
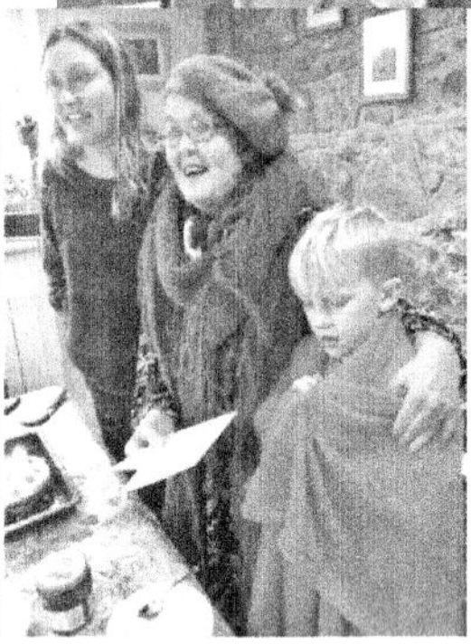

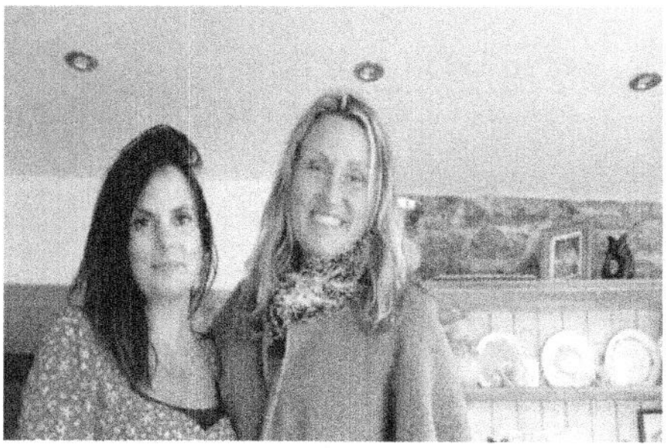
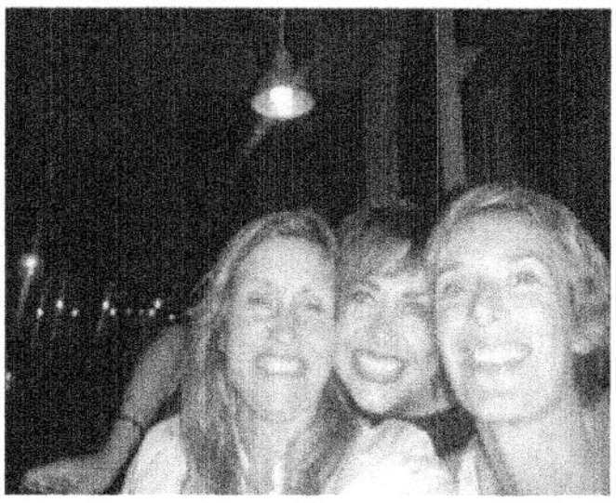
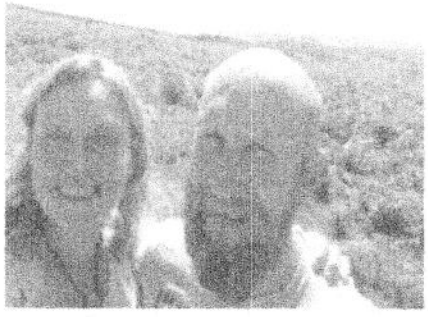
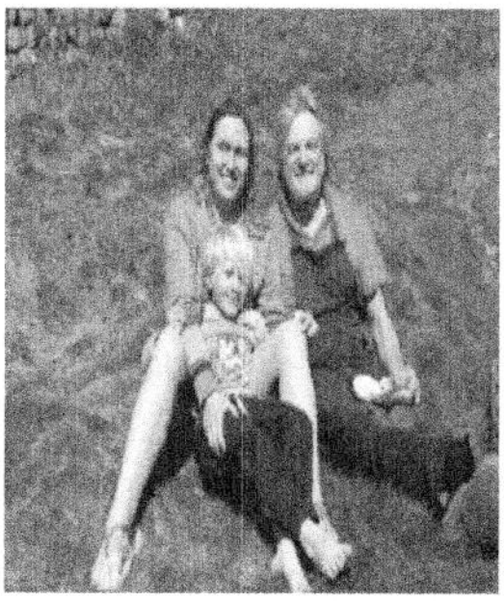
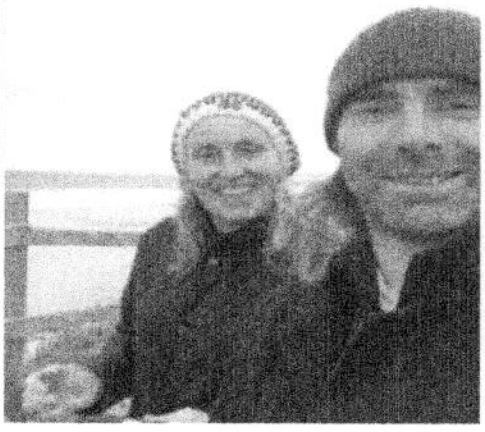
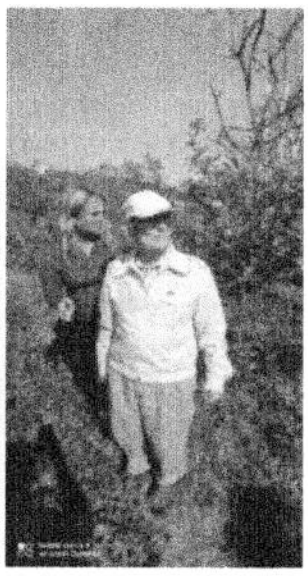

A little Play List from this book

Roo Panes 'Little Giant'

Joan Armatrading 'Love And Affection'

Billie Eilish 'Come Out And Play.'

Kate Bush...... Prologue Aerial.

And 'A Sky Of Honey.'

Sean Mendes 'In My Blood.'

Nick Drake 'Northern Sky.'

Leonard Cohen 'Famous Blue Raincoat.'

Tears For Fears 'Everybody Wants To Rule The World.'

Hold tight my brave warrior because happiness is within you and you will find her.

Printed in Great Britain
by Amazon